Flying Helicopters

A Companion to the PPL(H)

Flying Helicopters

A Companion to the PPL(H)

Helen Krasner

Airlife

First published in 2011 by
Airlife Publishing, an imprint of
The Crowood Press Ltd
Ramsbury, Marlborough
Wiltshire SN8 2HR

www.crowood.com

British Library Cataloguing-in-Publication Data
A catalogue record for this book is available from the British Library.

ISBN   978 1 84797 271 2

Disclaimer
Please note that the author and the publisher of this book are not responsible
in any manner whatsoever for any error or omission, or any loss, damage, injury,
adverse outcome, or liability of any kind that may result from the use of any of
the instructions/information contained in this publication, or reliance upon it.
The information contained in this book is believed to be correct at the time of
publication but terms, details and conditions are constantly subject to change
by the relevant authorities. All material relating to the Private Pilot Licence
(Helicopters) should be checked against the Civil Aviation Authority
publication *LASORS*.

Typeset by SR Nova Pvt Ltd., Bangalore, India

Printed and bound in China by Leo Paper Products Ltd.

CONTENTS

GLOSSARY

This includes terms and abbreviations used in this book, as well as others that you may run into in other books and during conversations with your instructor or other pilots.

AAIB: Air Accidents Investigation Branch
AGL: Above Ground Level
AME: Aviation Medical Examiner
ASI: Air Speed Indicator
ATC: Air Traffic Control
ATCO: Air Traffic Control Officer
ATPL: Air Transport Pilot's Licence
AUW: All-Up Weight; the maximum weight at which the helicopter should be operated
CAA: Civil Aviation Authority
Circuit: the official flight pattern when close to the airfield
C of G: Centre of Gravity
CPL(A): Commercial Pilot's Licence (Aeroplane)
CPL(H): Commercial Pilot's Licence (Helicopter)
D & D: Distress and Diversion
DI: Direction Indicator
DR: Dead Reckoning
EOL: Engine-Off Landing
ETA: Estimated Time of Arrival
FI: Flight Instructor
FREDAH: Mnemonic for checks done during circuit details: Fuel, Radio, Engine, Direction, Altitude, Hatches/Harnesses
FREDHATT: Mnemonic for checks when departing from/returning to the airfield: Fuel, Radio, Engine, Direction, Hatches/harnesses, Altitude, Trim, Transponder
HASEL: Mnemonic for checks used when doing some manoeuvres: Height, Airspeed, Security, Engine, Location/lookout
HEMS: Helicopter Emergency Medical Service
HIGE: Hover In Ground Effect
HOGE: Hover Out of Ground Effect
IFR: Instrument Flying Rules
IMC: Instrument Meteorological Conditions
IR: Instrument Rating
Knots (kt): Nautical miles per hour; 1kt is approximately 1.1mph (1.8km/h)

LPC: Licence Proficiency Check

LTE: Loss of Tail Rotor Effectiveness

MAP: Manifold Air Pressure; a measurement of engine power

MAYDAY: Emergency radio call

NOTAMs: Notices to Airmen

PAN: Urgency radio call

PIC: Pilot In Command

POH: Pilot's Operating Handbook

PPL: Private Pilot's Licence

PPL(A): Private Pilot's Licence (Aeroplane)

PPL(H): Private Pilot's Licence (Helicopter)

PPR: Prior Permission Required (i.e. to fly to an airfield)

QFE: Altimeter setting to give the height above a particular airfield

QNH: Altimeter setting to give the height above mean sea level

RPM: Revolutions Per Minute

RRPM: Rotor Revolutions Per Minute

Skills Test: Final flying test taken in order to get a PPL

Squawk code: Radar code given to an aircraft by ATC for identification

TRT: Total Rotor Thrust; the lift that enables a helicopter to fly

Ts and Ps: Aircraft temperatures and pressures

VFR: Visual Flight Rules

VMC: Visual Meteorological Conditions

VNE: Maximum permitted airspeed

VOR: VHF Omnidirectional Range; a type of radio navigation system for aircraft

VSI: Vertical Speed Indicator

INTRODUCTION

There are plenty of books about helicopters, and quite a number of those are aimed at people who are undertaking the Private Pilot's Licence (Helicopter) course, the PPL(H). So why do we need another one? Does the poor student, already weighed down with books on principles of flight, navigation, meteorology and a host of other important subjects – to say nothing of assorted items of flying paraphernalia – really need yet another book?

I suspect that he or she does. For, in all this wealth of aviation material, I think that one thing is missing. I have never seen a book that explains in simple terms how the PPL(H) course actually works and what to expect from it. For example, there is nothing that tells the new student what he or she really needs to do before starting to learn to fly. And there is no book, to my knowledge, that goes through each exercise in the syllabus, explaining what it is about, why it is taught in the way it is, and how you can expect to feel when learning it.

It is equally hard, if not more so, to easily find the answers to the many questions that students tend to ask their qualified pilot friends – if they actually know anyone who flies – or possibly their instructor, if the two are on friendly terms outside of flying sessions. These include topics such as why hovering is so horribly difficult, the reasons for going solo fairly early in the course but why it might take one person far longer than another, and why learning to fly accurately is so important. Why, the student might ask himself, is it taking me so much longer than the theoretically required 45 hours to learn to fly a helicopter? Why are we spending so much time going over what each control does, when I feel as though I can manage to use all three together, and I don't want to waste time and money? Why are there so many exercises to do with emergencies? Why on earth do we practise flying circuits as aeroplanes do, when helicopters can land almost anywhere? And, perhaps most importantly for many: can I do this? Am I good enough? Will I make it?

This book will hopefully provide the answers to these types of questions and more. Based to a large extent on my own experiences, both as an instructor and from my memories of learning to fly helicopters myself, it is targeted at all those doing the PPL(H) course or considering undertaking it in the future. And it will hopefully fill in those perceived gaps that many people find are there, even after they have passed the Skills Test and acquired that coveted PPL(H).

The author with an R22 helicopter.

The first chapter of this book aims both to provide the basic knowledge that is needed before starting on the flying course, and also to answer some of the questions that people ask at this point. It includes an extremely simple introduction to helicopter principles of flight, and I apologize in advance to those for whom this stuff is obvious, who may feel they are being treated like children. However, while some people are rotary aviation addicts who will have read everything they could lay hands on about helicopters before starting to learn to fly one, others sign up for the course with no prior knowledge whatsoever. Having been one of the latter, I know now that a little advance preparation would have been useful!

After the first chapter, the rest of the book follows the order of the PPL(H) course. My hope is that students can read the relevant chapter before they have flown the corresponding exercise, at the point of coming to do it and also afterwards, probably getting something different out of it each time. The early chapters will assume no theoretical or practical knowledge at all, while the later ones will expect the student not only to have done some flying, but also to have learned some of the theory involved, as this is likely to be the case. This approach may bore some readers and leave others bemused at different points, but there is no way to pitch a book such as this at the perfect level for everyone all the time. All types of people, of all ages and from a variety of backgrounds, learn to fly helicopters – all I can do is try to aim this book at the majority of them.

The book will also cover some of the so-called 'human factors' aspects of the course. By this I mean topics such as why at some stages flying can be

10

difficult and demoralizing as well as enjoyable and great fun. People who struggle with flying training – and I suspect this is everyone at some stage – can sometimes feel very alone. Hopefully this book will help by explaining what is happening and that such feelings are common.

Of course, I should emphasize that I don't aim to actually teach anyone to fly a helicopter through reading this book, or to take the place of a flying school and a good instructor. I just want it to be something into which PPL(H) students can dip time and time again, always finding something that is useful or that strikes a chord with them. If that happens, I will have achieved what I set out to do.

I sincerely hope that you enjoy all that follows and find it useful. Flying helicopters is wonderful and a great privilege, so ensure that you make the most of it. And, above all, fly safely!

Flying helicopters is a great privilege.

1 Before Starting the PPL(H) Course

CHOOSING A FLYING SCHOOL AND INSTRUCTOR

Some people decide to learn to fly after having a 'trial lesson', sometimes referred to as an 'air experience flight'. If you haven't yet done this, I would suggest that you do, simply to ensure that you actually like flying helicopters. Watching helicopters fly, or being a passenger in one, is not at all the same thing as getting your hands on the controls. Most people love it; indeed, some become hooked and sign up for the course after an air experience flight that had been intended to be a one-off! But a few don't enjoy it, so you do need to ensure you aren't one of these.

Once you've decided that you like flying helicopters, the next thing to decide is where you are actually going to do your PPL(H) course. Some individuals just go to the flying school or club closest to their home, without further thought. There is something to be said for this. If you intend to travel on the day to each lesson, rather than doing a residential course, you really don't want to be too far from home. Flying can be exhausting, especially in the early stages, and you may find that a helicopter lesson combined with a long drive is just too much for you to cope with. Also, light aviation of any type is very weather-dependent, and you are likely to have a certain number of wasted journeys to the airfield, at least early on in your course. You really don't want to drive for three hours, only to be told that the weather has changed so you can't fly, leaving you with a three-hour drive home again. I learned at a school about one and a half hour's drive from my home, and I'd really consider that to be about the practical limit for most of us.

However, it is not always a good idea simply to choose the school closest to home, or the first one at which you flew. After all, you are about to spend a large sum of money on learning a complicated skill. You don't want to pay over the odds and, perhaps more importantly, you want to go somewhere where you'll feel comfortable and be well taught. So, as with any other large purchase, perhaps some market research would be a good idea. Therefore I suggest that you visit a few helicopter schools before making your final decision.

What are the other important factors to consider? For most people cost – generally quoted in terms of a price per hour for flying lessons – is a major issue. Indeed, some people simply call up a few flying schools, then pick the one which gives them the cheapest quote. This is not a good idea because, where flying hours are concerned, 'price per hour' does not tell the whole story. Find out how that hour is charged: some schools start the official 'hour' when the engine starts, others when the helicopter actually lifts off the ground. This may not make a great deal of difference for one individual lesson, but it will affect what you actually pay over the duration of the course, and to quite a large extent. Also, at a more crowded flying school, perhaps one based at a large airport, you may have to wait, with your engine running ('turning and burning'), until Air Traffic Control (ATC) allows you to fly: if you are being charged from engine start, this may make quite a difference to the final cost of the course.

Be very careful if a school quotes you a price for the whole PPL(H). This will usually be based on the legal minimum course flying time of 45 hours, and the majority of people take longer than that to get their licences. We may all think and hope that we're going to be natural pilots who do everything in minimal hours, but it's highly unlikely unless you're very young and have also had previous flying experience or learned something requiring similar co-ordination skills. The UK average for the PPL(H) is said to be 60–70 hours, so it is better to budget for about that amount. And finally, remember that if something seems too cheap, then as with anything else, quite possibly it is. You may indeed be getting a bargain, but you need to look into it carefully.

Next, you should decide if you are going to learn on an occasional basis, such as one lesson per week or one per fortnight, as most people do, or if you want to fly on an intensive course over a period of a few weeks. There are advantages to learning intensively: you may be able to do the whole thing in fewer flying hours, as you are less likely to forget things and have to go over exercises again. It also means you can learn at a flying school further from home, finding somewhere to stay locally. However, some people find intensive courses stressful and tiring. Personally, I do very badly on them, as I find that I need breaks to assimilate what I've learned, and you don't get that if flying very frequently. It really depends on the individual involved, so work out which is best for you and your personality. Also, flying is dependent on the weather and the British weather is not reliable, even in the summer. It is not unknown for students to book a three- or four-week course and find that it takes six weeks, or even doesn't happen at all. So if you go down the intensive course route, do so with your eyes open.

Some prospective students decide to overcome some of these problems by training abroad. It can certainly be cheaper to learn in countries such as the USA, South Africa, Australia or New Zealand. However, make sure that the qualifications you obtain at the end of the course will be accepted in the UK if that is where you intend to fly afterwards. Also, calculate carefully the cost of accommodation, airline flights, visas and the like, bearing in mind that the course may take longer than you expect – bad weather can happen anywhere, after all! Finally, remember that you will need to have some extra training when you return to the UK, to learn about flying in British weather conditions, UK radio use and so on. You might well find that the cost saving is negated when you factor in all of these.

One real problem with learning abroad is that you are unlikely to be able to visit the school in advance. It is always a good idea to do this if you possibly can, for all sorts of reasons. Cost is not everything; it is far more important to learn somewhere where you feel comfortable, where you like the atmosphere and the people. You are going to be spending a lot of time there, so make sure it is a place where you will be happy. This is difficult to establish without spending some time there, so be prepared to visit several schools if necessary, maybe even having trial lessons at all of them. It could be money well spent in the long run.

Another factor that is important for some people is the type of helicopter on which they will be learning. For most individuals it really doesn't matter that much. There are differences between helicopter types, but all of those generally used for training are suitable, and it is quite easy to convert from one to another after you have finished the course, should you wish to do so. But there are a few exceptions to this. If you weigh over 240lb (about 17 stone, or 108kg), you will be above the seat weight limit for the most common training helicopter, the Robinson R22, and if you are very tall you may find this particular helicopter rather cramped. In either case, you would probably be better off learning in some other type, such as the Robinson R44, Schweizer 300CBi or Enstrom 280. If this applies to you, look for a school that uses these helicopters, as the R22 is the only training helicopter available in a number of flying schools.

What about choosing your instructor? If you liked the instructor with whom you had your trial lesson, it could be a good idea to ask to stay with that person for the rest of your training, if that is possible. It is very important to

Which type of helicopter should you learn on?

get on well with the person who is teaching you to fly, for you will be spending a great deal of time with him or her, much of it in a cramped cockpit, and a personality clash would be a recipe for disaster. This is probably far more important than the experience level of the instructor, or whether he or she is old or young, male or female. New students often want to learn with the Chief Flying Instructor or the most experienced person around, but this is really not necessary. Often the newer instructor, who remembers learning to fly and can empathize with the student, and who is also full of enthusiasm, can be at least as good as the perhaps rather jaded chap who's been teaching people to fly for most of his life. This is one area where gut feeling is one of the most important factors; if you like someone, see if you can have them for your whole course. If you find that you have to fly with someone else it may not matter that much, so long as you can stay with the same instructor for most of your lessons. But if you find that you have to keep changing instructors every time, to the point where you get confused and find it hard to learn, perhaps you should find somewhere else to do your training. This occasionally happens, and is one reason why it is best to pay for each lesson as you go, rather than taking advantage of a small discount by paying for the course in advance, as is possible at some flying schools. The chance to remain totally flexible and change schools if you need to for any reason is very important.

Finally, remember that you are actually the best judge of where is a good place for you to learn to fly. Different things are important to different individuals, but everyone knows what is right for them. I had a student who came to the school at which I was teaching specifically because it was small and friendly, even though we operated out of a Portacabin at the time and didn't have many facilities. She had been to a larger school with expensive premises and she hadn't liked it. 'I didn't feel comfortable there', she explained, 'It wasn't right for me.' It was a good decision; she came to us and she got on well. So if you don't like a flying school for any reason whatsoever, go elsewhere. Find a school and instructor that you like and then enjoy learning to fly.

It is important to get on well with your instructor.

THE LENGTH OF THE FLYING COURSE

According to the official rules 'An applicant for a PPL(H) shall have completed at least 45 hours' flight time as a pilot of helicopters.' 'At least' are the important words here. This 45 hours is just a legal minimum, and it should be understood that the majority of people training for a private helicopter licence take longer than this, in some cases much longer. Yet somehow, over the years, that figure of 45 flying hours has become set in stone, as it were. People assume that the course takes 45 hours, no more and no less. Prospective students often think that it will definitely take them exactly 45 hours to complete the course, and some flying schools – who should know better – often quote a price for this amount of flying time. A legal minimum requirement is just that: it assumes that you are a natural pilot, learning under ideal conditions. Under such circumstances, it probably would take you 45 hours. But in practice that is very rarely the case.

Helicopters are very different from aeroplanes.

There are several reasons why the course usually takes longer than 45 hours. Firstly, the helicopter PPL is based on the fixed-wing equivalent – with as far as possible the same flying exercises and in roughly the same order – so the same number of flying hours is legally required. It's as though someone looked at the course for aeroplanes and said 'Let's make helicopters as similar as we possibly can'. But helicopters are different, and flying them is more difficult. So the PPL(H) is likely to take longer, though students doing the PPL(A) for fixed-wing aircraft frequently take longer than 45 hours, too.

Aptitude will certainly play a part and, generally, the younger you are, the quicker you learn, although there are exceptions to this rule. But many other factors are relevant, too. Usually, those learning on an intensive course over a period of a few weeks will pick up flying more quickly than those learning over a longer period of time. They forget less, and less time is spent repeating lessons and going over things again. The weather is also an important issue because if, like many students, you plan to have one or two lessons each week, it will take you the best part of a year to learn to fly. That means part of your course will be done over winter, and there may be days or even weeks when the weather simply isn't suitable. Long breaks from flying mean that students become rusty, and you will undoubtedly have to go over various exercises again. It is nobody's fault, and there is little that can be done about it. But that is the way it is.

Also, flying involves a large number of different skills, and students are rarely good at all of them. Those who pick up the actual flying fairly easily may struggle with navigation, and vice versa. Some people have a hard time learning to use the radio. Others find certain flight exercises difficult, sometimes for no obvious reason. Each person's flying course is individual, and so therefore is the rate at which they learn.

There will be days when the weather isn't suitable.

So how long does the course actually take for most students? Different figures are given for the national average, but it is often said to be between 60 and 70 hours. However, an average is just that, with some people learning faster and others taking longer periods of time. It is not unusual for students to take 80 to 90 flying hours, and hours into three figures are not unknown. At one school where I was an instructor there was a young man who really struggled with the course and also had to work away quite frequently, so that he sometimes had long gaps between lessons. He was told fairly early on that he was likely to take over 100 hours to get his licence. There is a great deal of individual variation, and it is difficult to estimate how long any student is likely to take. People frequently ask instructors for a personal estimate, but it really is impossible to say, and I would rarely hazard a guess at how long it will take anyone to complete the course.

Does it really matter how long it takes? As far as the flying is concerned, no, it doesn't matter at all. It may be a problem if you are short of money, that is all. But the time taken to get the PPL(H) says nothing whatsoever about whether someone is a good or bad pilot. It is just that some people learn more quickly than others. Also, being a competent pilot has much more to do with your attitude to flying, maturity, decision-making skills and knowledge of your limitations. Learning to fly and getting the PPL is only part of the whole picture, and after you get your licence, you are unlikely ever to be asked how long it took you to do so.

Individual schools differ when it comes to the average amount of time it takes them to get students through the course. It is not that one school is better than another. It may be that it takes longer at some airfields than others because, as mentioned earlier, at large airports more time may be spent waiting for other traffic. Also, some schools like to teach students things that are not officially part of the PPL(H) course, perhaps going beyond what is legally required. They do this from a safety point of view, and since you can never have too much knowledge, this is to be recommended.

Finally, bear in mind that doing the course in minimal hours is not necessarily a good thing. I have met pilots who did the PPL(H) in 45 hours, and some of them afterwards felt that they had been rushed and that further training would have been an advantage. I have met others who took longer, who worried at the time about how many hours it was taking them, but who realized afterwards that this was actually a big advantage in that they had learned more about helicopters than they would otherwise have done. There are many factors to take into account, and it is a complicated business.

Therefore, if at all possible, don't be concerned about how long it is going to take you to get your PPL. When comparing flying schools, if one tells you that they will get you through the course in 45 hours, take this with a pinch of salt. Your PPL will take as long as it needs to take for you. That is the best way, indeed the only way, to look at it. The actual number of flying hours is completely irrelevant.

THE ORDER OF THE FLYING EXERCISES

Some students start the helicopter flying course with very little prior knowledge of flying. They are happy to leave everything to the instructor; after all, this is what he or she is paid for! Others, however, prefer to know as much as possible in advance, and if you are reading this book it is highly likely that you are one of these. This means that you may by now have taken a look at the flying syllabus to see exactly what is involved in the PPL(H) course. If this is the case, you will have seen that the flying is divided into twenty-seven exercises, as follows:

Exercise 1: Familiarization with the Aircraft
Exercise 2: Preparation for Flight and Post-Flight Actions
Exercise 3: Air Experience Flight
Exercise 4: Effects of Controls
Exercise 5: Attitude and Power Changes
Exercise 6: Level Flight, Climbing, Descending and Turns
Exercise 7: Basic Autorotations
Exercise 8: Hovering
Exercise 9: Take-Offs and Landings
Exercise 10: Transitions
Exercise 11: Circuits
Exercise 12: First Solo
Exercise 13: Sideways and Backwards Flight
Exercise 14: Spot Turns
Exercise 15: Vortex Ring Recovery
Exercise 16: Engine-Off Landings
Exercise 17: Advanced Autorotations
Exercise 18: Forced Landings
Exercise 19: Steep Turns
Exercise 20: Precision Transitions
Exercise 21: Quickstops
Exercise 22: Navigation
Exercise 23: Advanced Take-Offs, Landings and Transitions
Exercise 24: Sloping Ground
Exercise 25: Limited Power Operations
Exercise 26: Confined Area Operations
Exercise 27: Instrument Flying

Many new students quite understandably expect the course to take place in precisely this order, and the exercises to be all of approximately the same length. Some people think that since they are charged by the hour, every lesson will take an hour. Indeed, I have been asked why, if there are twenty-seven exercises, the course takes 45 hours or more.

This is an entirely logical way of thinking, and is in fact a sensible question. However, it is not the case that all exercises take the same amount of time – far from it. Some exercises are far, far longer than others. Exercise 4, the Effects of Controls, is likely to take an hour, or perhaps a little less, although this does depend to some extent on the individual instructor and student. Exercise 5 will probably take the same amount of time, but Exercise 6 covers a vast amount of information and takes much longer. Navigation is another topic that will be covered during several sessions, starting with trips within the local area, then gradually flying further and further afield. Some exercises, such as hovering, will generally be taught in periods of a few minutes or so over several sessions, although this does vary from school to school and instructor to instructor.

Navigation trips could involve flying further afield.

To make matters even more complicated, you are highly unlikely to do the flying exercises in the exact order presented here. Some students get confused when they are taught the basic effects of controls in the first lesson, then told to mark this in their log books as Exercise 4. What happened to Exercises 1, 2 and 3, they wonder. Well, Exercises 1 and 2 are purely theoretical, and are therefore often taught in odd moments between flying sessions, or perhaps on a rainy day when no flying is possible. And Exercise 3, the Air Experience Flight, is frequently the trial lesson which the student had before taking the plunge and starting the actual course – and you may well have it in your log book under 'Trial Lesson'.

During the later parts of the course, you will find that there is no 'correct' order for most of the exercises, and that you may not do things in the same way as the next student with whom you compare notes. To a certain extent this depends on the preferences of individual schools and instructors. Everybody teaches slightly differently, for all sorts of reasons. It is not that one method is right and another wrong; it is simply that there are different ways of doing things.

Furthermore, the so-called 'correct' order doesn't really work for some parts of the PPL(H) course. This is probably partly because the syllabus is based on the fixed-wing flying equivalent, and helicopters are different. While it may seem logical in theory for hovering to be a separate exercise, for someone writing a syllabus at any rate, in practice that doesn't work very well: learning to hover is exhausting in the early stages, and almost no-one could manage an hour of it. Hovering is therefore frequently taught in short sessions of ten minutes or so, perhaps at the end of other exercises. Another reason for doing this may be to add variety to the lessons, or simply to make a lesson up to an hour if the relevant information of the exercise in hand has been taught in a shorter time. Or it may simply be because of the weather. You can't fly at altitude if the cloud base is low or it's misty, but you can probably practise hovering . . . so that is what you do.

The weather is the reason for a large number of changes in the order of the syllabus. Exercise 7, 'Basic Autorotations', needs to be done at a height of over 2,000ft above the ground. If you can't get that high without going into cloud, your instructor will pick another exercise for that day. You need very light winds for 'Advanced Transitions' in Exercise 23, so you may have to do something else while waiting for the right conditions. Navigation requires good visibility, particularly in the very early stages, so if the weather is hazy you may find yourself doing more advanced manoeuvres that are close to the ground and the airfield. And so it goes on: it is simply a case of being practical.

Some students become quite worried about these changes to the order of the course. They fret in case they are leaving something out, or, conversely, that they are taking too long over a particular part of the course. Don't worry! Your instructor will make sure that everything is covered, no matter what order you do it all in. Having said that, knowledge of the course, and keeping track of what you have done and which exercises you still have left to do, is no bad thing. This is particularly the case if you find that you can't have the same instructor for the whole course, or if you have changed flying schools part-way through your flying training; in such circumstances things can occasionally get left out. It is never too early to take responsibility for your own flying, so keep notes of what you have done, and what you feel you have left to do.

'GOING SOLO' AND SOLO CONSOLIDATION FLYING

Many non-flyers think that 'going solo' comes right at the end of the flying course, after you've learned everything that you need to know. After all, when learning to drive a car, you're not considered safe to be alone at the controls of a car until you've passed your driving test, and you probably wouldn't expect to be. So why should flying be any different? In flying training – for any kind of aircraft – however, 'going solo' and flying alone afterwards are things that happen fairly early on in the course. Indeed, in fixed-wing aircraft, some students do their first solo flight after only a few hours' instruction. And they certainly aren't ready to do more complicated manoeuvres or pass their final flight test at this point.

Since the magic words 'flying hours' have come up again, let's get one thing straight. The number of hours it takes you to 'go solo' is irrelevant. It really, *really* doesn't matter how long it takes you to get to the point of your first solo flight. I emphasize this because people who are learning to fly can become obsessed with the concept of 'hours' and how many of them it's taken to get to a certain point in the course. The fact is that it takes different people varying amounts of time to go solo, and the reasons for this will be discussed at greater length in Chapter 3. For now, simply don't agonize about it.

The point I want to make, however, is that at some point, probably fairly early on in the course, your instructor will get out of the helicopter and you will be allowed to do a small amount of flying alone. Most often you will be asked to take off, fly one circuit of the airfield, and land. However, at some flying schools you may do a 'hover solo' first, when you just lift off, hover, and land. At still other places you may do more than one circuit of the field.

You will go solo when you've reached a point at which you can basically handle the helicopter competently. That is, you can lift it off the ground, hover, hover-taxi to where you want to go, climb, turn, level off, descend and land. Your instructor knows that you are able to do all of that safely, so he or she gets out of the helicopter and lets you prove it. Sometimes you may have to wait longer due to the weather, because you haven't yet got an aviation medical certificate (*see* Chapter 3), or simply because your instructor is a cautious type, but this is usually how it all works.

You will go solo when you can handle the helicopter competently.

Unlike when learning to drive a car, going solo is not the end of your flying training. If you think about it, perhaps that should be the case when learning to drive a car as well. After all, most people who pass the driving test still have a lot to learn: they probably know nothing about driving on motorways or narrow country lanes, they most likely haven't been taught how to drive in fog, and they may not know how to find their way by reading a map. They almost certainly won't have learned about driving in snow or correcting skids, or what to do in the event of some mechanical failure.

The difference is that in a car it isn't really crucial to know all these things, since if something goes mechanically wrong, or you're lost, or you're simply confused by the amount of traffic or the weather conditions, you can stop at the side of the road. You can phone a mechanic, or ask for directions, or wait till the weather gets better. You can even abandon your car and walk. But in a helicopter you can't do these things. You're on your own up there, and you need to be able to cope safely with anything that happens. Of course, unlike in most other aircraft you can land in a field if necessary, but you need to have had some instruction to do even that safely.

For this reason, learning simply to manage the controls is actually quite a small part of helicopter training. Therefore, after going solo you will start to do some of the more advanced stuff, roughly equivalent to what the new car driver learns on his own. You will learn how to land safely if the engine fails, and what to do in other emergencies. You will be taught how to navigate using an aviation chart, and the procedures you need to use when departing from or arriving at an airfield. You will master more advanced helicopter manoeuvres – though perhaps not as advanced as that shown in the photograph! You will learn how to land in a small area or on sloping ground – very useful for when you want to visit friends and park on their property or land at a restaurant or hotel. You will practise manoeuvring the helicopter more accurately, hovering sideways and backwards if necessary, and how to stop quickly if you need to. You will also have instruction on how to use some of the instruments that most helicopters have, to enable you to get out of trouble in bad weather … and on how to make a precautionary landing if the weather really closes in on you.

You will learn more advanced manoeuvres. (Neil Harrison)

Interspersed with all this will be what is known as 'solo consolidation flying'. That is, between formal flying lessons and when the weather is suitable, you will have the opportunity to go off on your own and do more solo flying. Generally 'make haste slowly' will be the maxim, and it's a good idea to remember that phrase throughout your flying career. So, having flown one circuit for your first solo flight, next time you might do three, then maybe fly alone for half an hour, then a little longer. You may have some solo hovering practice sessions. As with everything in the course, the details will differ, and instructors vary in what they want their students to do.

Later, having learned a little about navigation, you will also undertake solo navigation flights. Again, you will start with something very simple, possibly just flying to points that you can see from the airfield. Later still, you will fly to other airfields alone, probably to places to which you have been previously with an instructor, at least at first. Overall, you will do quite a lot of solo flying, since you need to have a minimum of ten hours of it before you can obtain your PPL(H).

What, you might ask, is the point of this solo consolidation flying? Wouldn't it be safer and more sensible for you to fly with an instructor the whole time until you'd passed your Skills Test, then go flying alone, after you've learned everything? There are good reasons for doing things the way they are done. For a start, that first solo flight is a tremendous confidence booster for most people. It proves to them that they can fly a helicopter, albeit only just! If all goes well, a student returns from his or her first solo with an ear-to-ear grin, and it is frequently something that is remembered for the whole of his life. Confidence is essential when flying – although over-confidence can be dangerous, but that's another story – so this is one good reason for letting students solo as soon as it is safe for them to do so.

Solo consolidation flying also has another purpose. It is a way of teaching students about decision-making, which is a tremendously important part of flying training. Decision-making – sometimes called captaincy – really cannot be learned while with an instructor; it has to be acquired alone. Some people can make airborne decisions naturally, but others find it quite difficult. I have had students who asked me every little thing when they were actually quite capable of deciding for themselves; it was a habit they had got into. For example, they might see that there was a hill ahead, and know how to put the helicopter into a climb, but still ask, 'Should I climb now?' One of my students would not even start the helicopter without asking me first, despite the fact that I had told him in advance to do so.

In effect, solo consolidation flying makes students 'grow up'. While the instructor is there with them, some people will always remain like children in a way, forever asking, constantly making sure, consistently leaning on that more experienced pilot sitting next to them, because they can. They need to learn to make their own decisions, to become helicopter pilots rather than perpetual students. Of course, you could eventually learn that by doing all or most of the course before flying solo, and occasionally it has to happen this way, for example if a student has a problem obtaining an aviation medical and his solo flying has to be delayed. It's not a major problem if that happens, but it's better if he can do it earlier and more gradually.

So accept your first solo and later solo flying simply as part of the course, and understand that flying alone is teaching you things that can only be learned by doing it that way. And, most importantly, enjoy it!

HOW HELICOPTERS FLY

It is quite possible to start the PPL(H) course with no knowledge whatsoever of rotary principles of flight. Just as you can learn to drive a car without knowing what goes on under the bonnet, so you can fly a helicopter without any comprehension of the technical details of how the aircraft works. This is just as well, for many helicopter students find this stuff incredibly difficult. For those with a scientific or engineering background there is usually no problem, but for the rest of us it can be quite baffling, and the vector diagrams that many instructors and textbooks delight in using at every opportunity only serve to confuse rather than enlighten. If this is you, I sympathize, for I've been there. Don't worry too much; you can learn to fly without understanding a great deal about how helicopters work. However, a little basic knowledge of the principles of flight is useful, and it will actually make it easier for you when you start the course. Later on you will be required to learn it in more detail anyway, in order to pass the ground exams required for the licence, so don't just skip this section. It is intended only to explain the basics of helicopter aerodynamics in very simple terms … and without a vector diagram in sight!

Many people think it is a complete mystery that helicopters manage to fly at all. They wonder how this bunch of noisy, whirling, vibrating parts manages to hurl itself into the air, never mind move under any semblance of control. Some of them reckon that a helicopter is like a bumblebee – it shouldn't be able to fly, but nobody told the bumblebee. Others – some pilots among them – think that helicopter aerodynamics is not only a complete mystery, but one they would rather leave well alone. After all, it's incredibly complicated, isn't it?

No, it isn't. While a helicopter is a far more complex machine than an aeroplane, the fundamental principles of flight are the same, and understanding the basics really isn't all that hard. To put it simply, the rotor blades of a helicopter are identical to the wings of an aeroplane, in that they are an aerofoil, which, when placed in an airflow, deflects the air in order to produce lift.

So what does this actually mean? It is simplest to visualize the airflow over a wing or rotor blade as a series of lines, as shown on the next page. When this airflow meets the wing, it splits so that some air flows above the wing and the rest below it. A cross-section of the wing, as illustrated, is called an aerofoil section. The curved shape of this aerofoil means that the air going above the wing has to accelerate in order for it to meet the air going under the wing at the far side of the aerofoil. When air speeds up its pressure decreases, so there is less pressure above the wing. Therefore lift is produced or, to put it another way, the wing is sucked up into the area of lower pressure. In fact, you can experience the same thing happening if you put your arm out of a car window when travelling along at a reasonable speed. Your arm acts as an aerofoil, lift is created, and you will find that it starts to be pulled upwards. The faster the airflow over the wing, the greater the lift produced. The amount of lift produced can also be changed by altering the angle at which the rotor blade meets the airflow; this is called the 'angle of attack'.

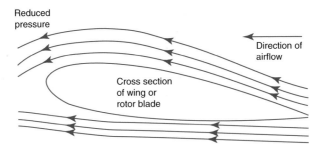

The airflow over a rotor blade.

An aeroplane creates this airflow over the aerofoil by accelerating along the runway until there is enough air going over the wings for the machine to start to fly. With a helicopter, the airflow is produced by rotating the 'wings' – the rotor blades – rather than by moving the whole aircraft. When the rotor blades start to spin, the air flowing over them produces lift in the same way as in an aeroplane moving forward. In the case of helicopters, this lift is usually known as total rotor thrust, or TRT. With an aeroplane, the lift is increased by going faster and faster along the ground. In the case of a helicopter, however, we increase the TRT partly by speeding up the blades and partly by altering their pitch – the angle at which they meet the airflow. This is done by raising a control lever in the cockpit called the collective lever. With any aircraft, when lift is greater than weight, the machine can fly, or in this case, lift into the hover.

However, there is a little more to it than that. With any aircraft, increasing the lift also means that there is more drag. Drag is the resistance to the passage of air – similar to wind resistance – and would slow down the rotor blades if nothing was done to prevent it. Therefore, when the collective is raised, the pilot needs to open the throttle to produce more engine power, in order to prevent the rotor blades from slowing down. There is a twist-grip throttle on the end of the collective for this purpose. But in most modern helicopters it is only used during start-up and shutdown; during flight an electronic governor monitors the rotor revolutions per minute (RPM) and adjusts the engine power as required. It's one less thing for the helicopter pilot to think about – for which most of us are very grateful.

So to lift the helicopter into the hover, the pilot starts the engine to get the rotor blades turning, then raises the collective to increase the TRT and lift the helicopter into the hover. However, this causes our next problem. As the blades turn in one direction, the fuselage will start to rotate in the opposite direction. This is a result of Newton's Third Law, which states that for every action there is an equal and opposite reaction. Another way of looking at this in everyday terms is to consider that you are sitting in a rowing boat by a river bank. If you push on the bank, the boat moves and is forced further out into the water. This is an example of Newton's Third Law. We don't want the helicopter to whirl around in circles, and the most common method of preventing that is to have a tail rotor. A small version of the main rotor, this is mounted vertically at the end of the tail cone, and works by pushing the tail back as the fuselage tries to rotate. It is like having a sideways rotor system to push the fuselage straight.

An added benefit of having a tail rotor is that it can also be used to control the helicopter in 'yaw', or movement about the vertical axis. This is done by altering the pitch of the tail rotor blades, and therefore the amount of lift – or in this case sideways movement – that they produce. Tail rotor pitch is controlled by the helicopter's 'yaw pedals'. They are not rudder pedals, as some fixed-wing pilots mistakenly believe, because although they move the aircraft in the same way, they act using different principles.

We can now lift the helicopter into the air with the collective lever and control it in yaw with the yaw pedals. But we also need to be able to move it forwards . . . and sideways and backwards, since one advantage of helicopters is that they can move in any direction. This is done by altering the direction of the TRT. When we lift into the hover, the TRT acts solely vertically. However, the cyclic control lever in the cockpit can alter the angle of the whole rotor system – what we call the 'rotor disc', the circular disc that the rotors make when they are turning. This is done by altering the pitch of each rotor blade by a different amount, but we really don't need to worry about the details of that here. In practice it means that if, for instance, the pilot moves the cyclic control forward, the rotor disc tilts forward. Total Rotor Thrust, instead of being solely vertical, now has a horizontal component, so the helicopter moves forward. But of course, you rarely get something for nothing. As some of the TRT is now being used to move the helicopter horizontally, the vertical component has been reduced and if nothing is done, the helicopter will start to descend. Therefore, in order to stay level, the pilot needs to raise the collective and add more power. But when he or she does this, the pitch angle of the tail rotor blades needs to be similarly increased, using the pedals, to prevent the helicopter yawing. Thus all the controls affect each other and their use needs to be co-ordinated – which is why to a beginner helicopter flying can seem so difficult.

There are other complications once we actually start to move the helicopter forward. In a steady hover in still air, the spinning rotor blades will all produce an equal amount of lift. However, once the helicopter starts to move forward, this is not the case. If you are moving forward at 10kt the advancing blade – that is, the blade moving into the direction of travel – has an airspeed of 20kt more than the retreating blade, which is moving in the opposite direction. To put it another way, if the rotor RPM is X knots, the advancing blade has an airspeed of X + 10kt, and that of the retreating blade is X – 10kt. The same applies if you are hovering in a headwind, since it does not matter if the airflow over the blades is increased by moving the helicopter or increasing the wind. Whether due to forward movement or to a headwind, this means that the advancing blade has more lift and, if nothing were done, the helicopter would roll sideways and crash.

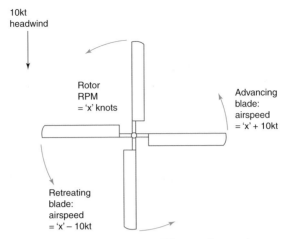

With a headwind, each blade position has different airspeed.

In fact, the very early helicopters did just this. As soon as they started to move forward they rolled towards the retreating blade side and turned over. The problem was eventually solved by looking at the autogyro, which had been invented in the 1920s by a Spaniard, Juan de la Cierva. Faced with the dilemma of trying to prevent his early machines rolling over and thrashing themselves to bits, Cierva discovered that if he made his blades flexible rather than rigid, so that they could flap up and down, everything worked just fine. Helicopter designers now did the same thing – they designed their rotors with a flapping hinge – and the flapping cleared up the dissymmetry of lift issue.

How does this work? With flexible blades, the advancing blade has more airflow and therefore more lift, so it flaps up. But as it climbs, it receives more of what is known as the 'induced flow'. This is a part of the airflow that is directed vertically downwards through the rotors as they turn. This induced flow reduces the lift the blade is actually producing, so it starts to fall, or flap down. As it flaps down, it receives less induced flow, and therefore less lift. Meanwhile, the opposite is happening with the retreating blade. This happens continually, with the blades continually flapping so that a state of equilibrium is reached, with lift over the whole rotor disc being equal. It's called, unsurprisingly, 'flapping to equality'.

So the pilot is now in a steady hover in a 10kt wind, and wants to leave the airfield. All he has to do is move the cyclic forward to tilt the rotor disc the way he wants to go, raise the collective so he doesn't start to descend, and correct the resulting yaw with the pedals, doesn't he? Well, not quite. Acceleration causes some other interesting aerodynamic effects. The first is called 'flapback', which is really a special case of flapping to equality. As the pilot moves the cyclic forward, the rotor disc tilts forward and downwards, and the helicopter accelerates. As it does this, the advancing blade flaps up, and the retreating blade flaps down, as explained in the previous paragraph.

However, the advancing blade reaches its highest point as it arrives at the front of the helicopter and the retreating blade gets to its lowest point at the back, so the rotor disc is now horizontal again. Therefore acceleration stops, as the disc has flapped back to its original position, so if the pilot wants to increase speed he has to continually move the cyclic forward. In fact, a small amount of forward pressure on the cyclic is always required. A small helicopter is unstable and has to be 'flown' continually, unlike a fixed-wing aircraft, which can be trimmed and then left alone with very little pilot input.

The next thing that happens is that at about 10–12kt of airspeed the helicopter will suddenly try to climb, all by itself. This is due to what is known as 'translational lift', which is effectively free lift – yes, occasionally you do get something for nothing. What is happening is that the increased speed means that less air is directed downwards through the disc; that is, there is less induced flow. As already stated, induced flow reduces lift, so now the helicopter has more lift, and it will start to climb, sometimes quite dramatically. So the pilot either needs to lower the collective, or move the cyclic further forward to convert the lift energy into speed. But translational lift only occurs once, while the speed is increasing – you don't get more of it as the helicopter goes faster. So after correcting for it initially as the helicopter speeds up, the pilot can then ignore it . . . until he comes to land and loses it when slowing down.

Putting all of this together, it is clear why flying helicopters requires a high degree of co-ordination and concentration, at least in the beginning. However, like learning to ride a bike, drive a car or acquire any other skill, practice makes perfect, and after a while the rotary flying student wonders just what was so difficult.

NOTES FOR CONVERTING FIXED-WING PILOTS

I had held a PPL(A) for around a year when I first tried helicopter flying. I had booked a rotary trial lesson just for something different to do, and I had absolutely no intention of taking it up. But that half hour changed my life: as soon as I tried hovering, I absolutely loved it and just knew that I had to do more. To be honest, I fought hard against the urge. I told myself it was too expensive, and that I couldn't possibly fly both fixed-wing and rotary aircraft safely, to say nothing of the time and money involved. At first, I booked only a couple more hours, telling both the instructor and myself that I'd just like to master the hover. Then I did a little more, then still more. It finally dawned on me that I was totally hooked on rotary aviation, and I wasn't going to stop. The rest, as they say, is history.

I'm certainly not unique – helicopter flying does tend to affect many people in that way. If you're reading this section, there's probably something about helicopters that grabs you. If you've already tried flying one you'll have some idea what the attraction is. In my experience, there's just something about being in charge of a machine that you have to control all the time, rather than an aircraft that basically flies itself as aeroplanes do. Hovering in a small helicopter is more like strapping on an extra part of your body rather than climbing into an aircraft. If you enjoy hands-on flying, you just can't help liking it. And, of course, there's the great visibility, the chance to slow down and look at things and the ability to land almost anywhere. There are lots of things to like about helicopter flying, and every year a certain number of fixed-wing pilots take a deep breath, talk nicely to their bank managers, and convert to helicopters.

Every year some fixed-wing pilots convert to helicopters.

However, if you've decided to do this, there are a few things you need to consider, since you are not in quite the same position as the complete beginner. Firstly, there's the time it will take you to learn. I probably wasn't unique in expecting to do my PPL(H) course in minimum hours. After all, I already knew how to fly. Converting fixed-wing pilots are allowed a small reduction in hours, and most of them are permitted – at least theoretically – to do the PPL(H) in 39 hours. I say 'most of them' because what the rule actually says is that 'holders of pilot licences … may be credited with 10 per cent of their total flight time as Pilot-in-Command in such aircraft up to a maximum of six hours towards a PPL(H)'. So if you have less than 60 hours as PIC, your credited hours will be correspondingly reduced. If you have a current PPL(A) you will also only have to pass two of the ground exams, Helicopter Principles of Flight and Flight Performance & Planning.

However, that six hours' reduction in the flying is usually somewhat theoretical. As already stated, very few people actually manage to qualify in minimum hours, and this applies equally to converting fixed-wing pilots, surprising though it may seem. Rotary aircraft are very different from aeroplanes, and the Robinson R22, on which most of us learn, is more difficult than most, being very light and responsive – or awkward and twitchy, as many frustrated students would probably put it, at least in the early days. It was originally designed for experienced helicopter pilots rather than as a training aircraft, and mastering it can take quite a lot of time and effort. It effectively means that helicopter students learning on the R22 rarely go solo in less than 20 hours, and often considerably more – it took me more than 30 hours to my first rotary solo flight. This is clearly more than many of their fixed-wing counterparts. So please don't get upset and frustrated if you've done around 15 hours' rotary flying, still haven't mastered the hover, and there's no mention of a first solo. It just means that you're normal!

The R22 is very light and responsive.

If you can afford it, and have access to them, if may be worth trying out other rotary aircraft before deciding which type you'd like to learn on. The R22's big brother, the four-seater R44, has considerably more space inside, which is useful for larger or heavier pilots, and it is a little easier to fly than the R22. Both the Schweizer 300CBi and Enstrom 280 are used as training aircraft, and are a little heavier and easier to fly than the R22. However, training in these other types tends to cost more than in the R22.

Is the ability to fly fixed-wing aircraft of any help to the prospective helicopter pilot and do the skills you've already learned transfer to this very different type of flying? Some most certainly do. If you have a PPL(A), you will be accustomed to being in the air, you know about navigation and you can use the radio. These things are much the same in all types of aircraft, and this will be a great help. However, you will find navigation in a light helicopter a bit of a challenge, since most small helicopters cannot be trimmed and so you cannot take both hands off the controls; therefore cockpit management and advance planning are things you will need to learn. On the other hand, in a helicopter you can slow down if you want to, which is very useful when you're navigating, as it gives you time to sort things out. This is something you cannot do in an aeroplane, of course. While coming to a high hover to look at your chart is not a good idea for all sorts of reasons, slowing down to 50–60kt is fine, since helicopters don't stall. Why shouldn't you come to a high hover? First, the helicopter becomes harder to control at very low airspeeds, and more susceptible to the effects of wind. But more importantly, at very low airspeeds you can occasionally encounter a dangerous phenomenon known as 'vortex ring'. This will be described in detail later on. However, at this point it is enough to understand that coming to a hover while distracted – i.e. looking at a chart – is not recommended.

What about the actual flying skills? Individuals vary, but most fixed-wing students converting to rotary flying find the upper air work relatively easy. The controls may be unfamiliar, but the way they work is not all that different. The cyclic controls your attitude and airspeed, the collective adjusts the height, and the pedals control the aircraft in yaw and keep it in balance. This general idea should sound reassuringly familiar, and while the R22 is likely to be twitchier than most other aircraft you have flown, mastering it at altitude probably won't take you that long.

Hovering, however, is a whole different ball game. It is quite unlike anything else in aviation, and many fixed-wing pilots struggle with it far more than they expected. This is not invariably the case as there are huge differences between individuals, and a number of PPL(A) holders manage to hover quite well very early on, even on a trial lesson. On my first helicopter flight, I succeeded in hovering using all three controls for 35 seconds – my instructor was timing it. He was amazed – or pretended to be – saying that I must be a natural pilot, and he'd never seen anyone pick it up that fast. But as an instructor, I have seen a number of fixed-wing pilots acquire the skill just as quickly.

However, some don't, and I've never been able to work out why. I think it has more to do with some people understanding the process of learning new skills rather than with any specific piloting aptitude. Some people have acquired the knack of relaxing and learning faster and some haven't. If it's any consolation to ex-fixed-wing pilots struggling to come to grips with the hover, it still seemed to take me as long as anyone else to actually get my PPL(H).

Then there are the specific helicopter exercises – autorotations, confined area landings, quickstops and out-of-wind operations. These will be completely new to the fixed-wing pilot, and are likely to take him or her as long as anyone else. The exceptions to this will probably be pilots with a great deal of experience of different types of aircraft, or those who have done aerobatics or similar skills. They will probably find something in their wide aviation repertoire to which they can relate the new manoeuvres, and so pick them up considerably faster.

Are there any disadvantages in having learned to fly fixed-wing aircraft first? Well, the Robinson Helicopter Company certainly thinks so. There is a supplement in the R22 Pilot's Operating Handbook, warning of the dangers of high hours aeroplane pilots flying helicopters. The problem can occur in an emergency, specifically in the case of engine failure. The first thing you do when an aeroplane engine fails is lower the nose to maintain flying speed, but you definitely don't want to do this in a light helicopter! You need to flare, which helps raise the rotor RPM, and it is this which keeps you flying. You then lower the collective and enter autorotation. It is the tendency of fixed-wing pilots to immediately lower the aircraft nose when it all goes quiet that prompted Robinson to publish this supplement. If you decide to fly both types of aircraft, this is something worth remembering. I decided that the best thing to do was to make sure that my automatic reactions were helicopter ones, since in an aeroplane you have a little more time in an emergency, and flaring slightly in an engine failure would not be catastrophic. If you do acquire both types of licence, but only fly helicopters occasionally, be very careful!

What about keeping both licences current? Unfortunately, you cannot count the hours on one type of aircraft towards the other; they are totally separate. For helicopters, you need to fly a minimum of two hours a year on every type for which you are rated, each helicopter type requiring a separate rating. You also need to do an LPC (Licence Proficiency Check) annually with an examiner, again on every type you fly. Some of the larger helicopter types are grouped together, but the details of these are not really relevant at this stage.

That's really about it. Now go out and book a trial helicopter lesson and get started on your PPL(H) course. It's tremendous fun, and I'm certain that you'll never regret it.

Now go and book a trial lesson.

2 PREPARATORY EXERCISES

EXERCISES 1–3

As already explained, there are twenty-seven exercises in the PPL(H) syllabus. Therefore you might logically expect to start at Exercise 1 and then go through them all in numerical order. However, it is unlikely to be what happens when it comes to helicopter training. Indeed, many students are quite puzzled when they do the 'Effect of Controls' as their first formal lesson, and are then told by the instructor to mark it as Exercise 4. The reason for this is that, as already noted, the first three exercises in the syllabus are not part of the formal flying course, but are preparation for it. Exercises 1 and 2 are mainly theoretical, and Exercise 3 is the so-called 'Trial Lesson' or 'Air Experience Flight'.

Exercises 1 and 2 are mainly theoretical.

EXERCISE 1: FAMILIARIZATION WITH THE AIRCRAFT

This first exercise covers points such as the external features of the helicopter, the cockpit layout, the aircraft systems, helicopter checklists and emergency procedures. It includes the aircraft's main and tail rotor systems, the fuel and oil systems, the electrical system and the radio equipment.

This summary is very short, but if you happen to have found a book that explains each exercise in detail, you might well find yourself panicking at the amount of information that you appear to be expected to acquire in this exercise! However, you don't need to get too apprehensive. In practice, Exercise 1 is not usually taught as a separate lesson; it is far more common for all the information to be covered over an extended period of time, so that you acquire the knowledge gradually. At the start your instructor may well simply show you the obvious external features of the helicopter, and explain how thing like the seat belts and doors work, and leave anything more complicated for later on. There is a lot to take in when starting to fly a helicopter, and trying to do it all at once would be too much for most people. It would lead to mental overload, when your brain can't cope with the amount of information being presented to it and simply refuses to take in any more.

The first exercise covers the external features of the helicopter.

Again, flying schools and instructors vary, but you are likely to be shown how to use a checklist fairly early on in the course, since checklists are common and very important in all types of flying. A checklist is simply what it says – a list of points that need to be covered for a particular activity. There is one for starting up the helicopter, another for shutting it down, and various ones for emergencies ... though the latter need to be learned by heart eventually, since you wouldn't have time to read them in a real emergency. Then you will be taught about the main helicopter controls and how they work. Next will probably come the instruments and dials in the cockpit, so that you can accurately identify them and know what they do. But you may not learn much of this until you have done some flying, so don't be concerned if that happens.

You will not need to know in a great amount of detail about the working parts of the helicopter such as the fuel, ignition and lubrication systems; that is the job of the helicopter engineer. However, as a pilot you will need to know a certain amount, perhaps more than many people realize at first. This is because, unlike in a car, if anything goes wrong when you are flying you can't just stop and phone the emergency services, so you need to have some idea of what is going on. For the same reason, we try to be sure that nothing does stop working during flight, and certain basic things such as the fuel and oil levels and emergency warning lights are checked before every flight. There is also a far more thorough check – the so-called 'A' check – that is done at the start of every day, and at some point you will be shown this more detailed way of checking over the helicopter … but strictly speaking this is part of Exercise 2, and I don't want to confuse you perhaps more than I have already! In practice, teaching the 'A' check is often saved for a rainy day when flying has to be cancelled at short notice; I have many memories of looking at the systems of a helicopter in great detail in a hangar, while rain poured down outside. Unless you have a technical background you may, as I did, find the 'A' check quite complicated and hard to remember; therefore it is a good idea to ask to go over it several times during the course, and indeed your instructor may well suggest this.

Exercise 1 also includes all the emergency procedures. This is a huge subject and a very important part of helicopter training. In practice, you will be learning about it throughout the flying course; the various topics should be drip-fed to you over time. Whichever helicopter you learn on, the Pilot's Operating Handbook (POH) for that type will explain in detail what you should do in the event of every conceivable type of emergency. If you can, try to get a copy of this document and use it constantly. At some flying schools the POH is easily available, but others seem to keep them under lock and key and practically expect you to sign the Official Secrets Act before you can have one. Persevere, as the POH is really useful, and you do need to learn about emergency procedures. Many of them, such as what to do in the event of engine failure, will be practised extensively during the course, while others will simply be learned about in theory.

It is not vital to know everything covered in Exercise 1 at the start of your course, but you must know it all by the time you finish. Because in practice this material tends to be taught in small sections throughout the course, it is important that you try to keep track of what you have been taught, and make sure that you are gradually acquiring all the knowledge that is required. It ought to happen without your intervention, and if you have the same instructor throughout your flying course, it probably will. However, sometimes it is necessary to change instructors, or even go to a different flying school partway through the PPL(H). If this happens, it is very easy for some small but important points to get left out, even though everyone is doing their best. Many pilots realize some time after qualifying that there are certain things they were never taught, and that is not ideal. The solution for this is to take responsibility for your own helicopter training early on. Try to find out what you should know, and if some of it is inadvertently being omitted, ask your instructor, or learn it yourself from the textbooks, or both of these.

EXERCISE 2: PREPARATION FOR FLIGHT AND POST-FLIGHT ACTIONS

This exercise is also theoretical. Its aim is to teach you the actions that are required to prepare you and the helicopter for flight, and the actions needed when the flight is completed. According to one handbook I have read, it consists of 'aircraft authorization, aircraft acceptance, external checks, internal checks, starting, engaging the rotor, running down and stopping the engine, leaving the aircraft, and completion of authorization and aircraft documents'.

Don't be disconcerted by the huge amount of information that is apparently required. As with aircraft familiarization, you will learn it all in stages. Early on, the aircraft authorization and acceptance, which is the paperwork required before a flight is permitted, will be completed by your instructor, since the signature of the pilot in command will be required; likewise for the paperwork required after flight. You will not be able to do it until at least after your first solo flight, and for some of it not until you have your pilot's licence.

You will also be taught the external and internal checks slowly and gradually. As already mentioned, there is a detailed 'A' check that is done on every aircraft before its first flight of the day, but certain important things such as the fuel and oil levels are looked at before every flight. The exact procedure varies slightly, depending on which type of helicopter you are learning on.

There are other things to be considered, such as the weather, what other aviation activities are going on in the local area, and the weight of the helicopter plus its occupants. Also, it is the job of the pilot to ensure that everyone is wearing suitable clothing, and of course that his health is good and he is fit to fly.

Next will come starting up the helicopter. You may be allowed to have a go at this from Day 1, but it is more likely that your instructor will do it until you become a little more accustomed to helicopter flying. However, this makes little difference. You will be following a checklist, doing exactly what it says, and in the correct order. This will probably seem rather complicated at first but, as with most new skills, it will become easier with practice. It helps to understand that basically it is broken down into three main sections: you check that everything is as it should be before starting the engine; you then start the engine and get the rotors turning; and when everything is ready for flight, you again check that there is nothing untoward occurring. Looking at it in this way should make the checklist seem less arbitrary – at least, I hope so!

When the flight is over, the pilot needs to get out his checklist again in order to shut down the engine. He then needs to make sure that the helicopter

Fuel and oil levels are checked before every flight.

is safely parked, and the procedures for this will vary at different flying schools. Again, these are things that will be done after every flight, and you will pick them up gradually.

In summary, Exercise 1 and 2 can ... be forgotten about! But this is not quite true. It is as well to know what they include, so that if at some point during the course you find that you really don't know as much about this side of things as maybe you should, you can do something to remedy it. But for now, let's get on with the actual flying.

EXERCISE 3: AIR EXPERIENCE FLIGHT

The so-called Air Experience Flight will be your first practical flying lesson, and it may well be the first time you have ever been in a helicopter. It is almost certain to be the first time you have tried handling helicopter controls. Some people will have this initial flight before they actually decide to take up helicopter flying, as a standalone 'trial lesson'. You might even have been bought a 'trial lesson voucher' as a present for a birthday or similar celebration. Indeed, this first flight may have been what got you hooked on the wonders of rotary flight in the first place, and made you decide to do more.

For most people the air experience flight is incredibly exciting. It is a completely new experience, and some individuals can be quite apprehensive and nervous, or even really scared. All sorts of worries go through people's minds. What will it be like? Is it safe? What happens if the engine fails? Will I be any good, or will I make a complete fool of myself? Will the instructor tell me I shouldn't even consider helicopter flying?

If any of this is you, stop worrying now! The air experience flight is just that – a chance to get the experience of being in the air in a helicopter. It is not a test, and it is not even a formal lesson as such. Its purpose is to give you the feel of flying a helicopter, so that by the end of the lesson you can make an informed decision as to whether you want to do more.

The chance to experience being in a helicopter.

That being the case, just relax and enjoy it. Will you be any good at it? No, the chances are that you won't, not at this stage. An air experience flight usually lasts 30 to 40 minutes – although you may have booked an hour – and absolutely no-one can learn to fly a helicopter in such a short period of time. Some people pick up new skills more quickly than others, so some individuals may initially find helicopter flying easier than others. But at this early stage, that doesn't mean a thing, one way or the other. I have had trial lesson students ask me after the flight if I think they'll be able to learn to fly. My answer is invariably yes, since to date I have never met any-one who can't learn to fly a helicopter, although I daresay such people exist, just as a few individuals can never pass a driving test. However, if they want to know how long it will take them, or how good they'll be, I'll really have no idea at that point. Some people struggle initially with flying, but later pick things up quite fast. Others appear to be 'naturals', but find more advanced exercises difficult. Still others simply learn slowly. I turned out to be one of those, so I sympathize, but we plodders get there in the end. Everyone learns in a different way, and it doesn't matter that much anyway. Once you are a pilot, no-one will ever ask you how long it took you to learn to hover. So just relax and enjoy the flight.

This first lesson will probably start with a briefing, although it may be quite short, and in some instances no classroom-type discussion takes place at all. This is not a problem, for the air experience flight is not a formal lesson, and in fact it is possible to teach everything required for it out in front of the heli-copter. While I normally include briefings for air experience flights, sometimes I decide to show people the helicopter controls on the actual machine rather than on the whiteboard, particularly if it is a nice sunny day. So don't feel short-changed if you don't have a formal briefing for this particular exercise.

However, you should get the opportunity to talk to your instructor, and this is important. For now is the time to discuss anything which is worrying you, such as extreme nervousness, a history of airsickness, or almost anything else you want to mention. It is also a good opportunity to say if there is anything you would like to do or have demonstrated during the lesson. Some people want to know what happens if a helicopter engine fails, and would like to experience a demonstration of simulated engine failure. Others can't think of anything more terrifying! Some people really, really want to have a go at hovering. Some trial lesson students live nearby and would like to fly over their houses, while others want to spend the whole time on the actual learning experience. Instructors aren't mind readers, so if there is anything you especially want, just ask. However, do bear in mind that in half an hour it may not be possible to fly to a student's house some distance away, take photos, do lots of flying and hovering, then demonstrate an engine failure – something may need to be left out. When you actually start the flight you will sit in the captain's or chief pilot's seat, which for most helicopters – though not all – is the right-hand seat. This is a way of emphasizing that you are now a pilot, albeit only one who is learning, not a mere passenger. However, don't get alarmed at this; all training helicopters have dual controls, and your instructor will be very experienced at flying the helicopter from the left-hand seat. He won't expect you to know what you're doing on a first flight!

Will you actually learn anything formal during this flight? Yes, you most definitely will. You will briefly be told the name of each control and what it does, although the detailed effects of the controls will not be explained in any detail. To put it concisely, the pilot holds the cyclic stick in his right hand, which will control the speed and attitude of the helicopter. His left hand will be on the collective lever, which controls height and power, the latter through a twist-grip throttle on the end. His feet will be on the pedals, which control the helicopter in yaw – turning about a vertical axis – and also keep it in balance. You may only get to try out one of these controls during your trial lesson, probably the cyclic, but that is often quite enough for a first sortie in an unstable aircraft.

Next, your instructor will go over the usual method for handing over control of the aircraft. All helicopters have dual controls, so it is essential to know who is flying the helicopter at all times. Someone needs to be handling the controls of an unstable aircraft like a helicopter, but your instructor won't let go of any control until he or she knows you have it. Similarly, you don't both want to be fighting to fly the helicopter! So you will learn when to use the phrases 'I have control', 'You have control', 'I have control of the cyclic', and so on, plus exactly what they mean. You will also learn to 'follow through' on the controls. This means that you hold the control while the instructor demonstrates something, applying enough pressure to be able to feel what is happening, but not enough to restrict his movements. You will most likely do this before having a go on the control yourself. If you can't feel anything happening when you're following through, it may be that you need to apply a little more pressure or it may simply be that helicopter control movements are tiny, particularly in the R22, and you aren't quite attuned to them yet. Don't worry: part of the reason for following through is to give you an idea of how little you actually need to move the controls and how responsive helicopters are.

This may be all that you will be formally taught, but you might also be asked to point out other aircraft that are nearby, using the clock code system. This means that you imagine a clock lying horizontally, with you at the centre. Then, for instance, if an aircraft is straight ahead but a little to the left, you might report it as at 'eleven o'clock', perhaps with the addition of 'high' or 'low' – i.e. above or below the horizon – for extra clarity. You may also have some of the local landscape and airfield features pointed out to you, so that you start to build up an idea of what the local area looks like.

Of course, you will have a go at flying the helicopter yourself, and possibly you will get to try hovering. You may find it all quite difficult, particularly hovering, but it will get easier with practice. Don't worry, don't get scared, and above all don't judge yourself. Some people think the instructor will be judging them, deciding whether they are good or bad, giving them points out of ten for performance. Believe me, he probably won't. He will simply be sitting there, ready to take control if it seems like a good idea, keeping the flight safe. Above all, his main aim will be to enable you to enjoy the flight. He is probably a helicopter enthusiast himself, and loves to introduce others to the wonders of rotary flight. Most helicopter instructors love flying and get on well with people, so they enjoy their work. Personally, I love doing trial lessons!

Probably more quickly than you would expect, the time will be up. Despite the fact that you may find yourself wanting to do more, it will probably be quite enough for your first helicopter lesson. In fact, you are likely to feel tired, though hopefully exhilarated too. The flight should also have given you an idea of whether you want to carry on – and hopefully you will. And if you haven't bought a personal log book yet, now is the time to do so, for the air experience flight is officially the first lesson of the course, and you can log it as such.

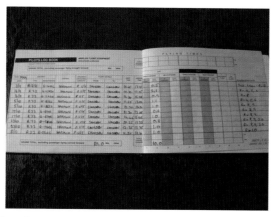

Buy a log book and record this first flight.

3 PRE-SOLO FLYING

EXERCISES 4–12

This is the beginning of the flying course proper, and your lessons should now follow a set pattern. Each one will start with a briefing, which will go over the important points of the flying exercise and some of the associated theory. You will probably find it helpful if you can manage to read up about the theory in advance, but it's not absolutely essential. The exercises will be done in approximately the order they are described here and in other books, but not necessarily exactly like that. Some exercises, such as hovering, are more likely to be done over a period of time, perhaps for ten minutes at the end of every flying session. The weather will also play a part, as sometimes conditions may be unsuitable for the scheduled lesson, so your instructor may decide that you will do something else. Therefore you need to be ready, be flexible and be prepared for anything.

These first lessons are very important, as they will lay down the foundations for your future flying. Habits learned at this early stage will be with you for ever, and if you are badly taught it can be quite hard to change things later on. It can be done, but it isn't easy and I speak from experience! Many people are desperate to get through the basics quickly, to go solo and then get on with what they perceive to be more exciting and important flying exercises. They shouldn't be. If you have an instructor who takes things steadily, gives detailed briefings, and is a stickler for detail and getting things right, you are very lucky. You have a good instructor, and you should hang on to him or her!

It should also be emphasized that what follows is not intended to take the place of your textbook or briefings. Its aim is simply to give you an idea of what to expect, and hopefully provide some useful information that you may not find from other sources.

EXERCISE 4: EFFECTS OF CONTROLS

This is the first formal lesson of the PPL(H) course. The briefing, which is fairly long, will go over each of the different flying controls and how they work. The flying exercise will then consist of your instructor demonstrating each control, and you then trying it for yourself.

First, the briefing. Instructors have something of a dilemma with Exercise 4. There is a lot of information to pass on, but some students clearly do not want to listen. They have probably waited a long time to learn to fly, and now they

You may do some hovering at the end of each session.

can't wait to do just that – fly! They want to learn about things in the air, not in front of the whiteboard. If this is you, please believe me when I say that briefings are extremely important. You need to understand how a helicopter works as well as teaching your hands and feet how to fly one. Flying intuitively is all very well, but the good pilots are those who also know what will happen, and why, before they move each control.

Cyclic Control

The cyclic – sometimes called the stick – controls the attitude and airspeed of the helicopter. Movement of the cyclic alters the tilt of the rotor disc, which is the hypothetical disc the rotors make when they are turning. The rotor disc is attached to the helicopter fuselage, so where it goes, the aircraft will have to follow. Therefore, if you move the cyclic forward, the helicopter will pitch nose-down, descend and increase in speed. Pulling back on the cyclic will cause the aircraft to pitch nose up, climb and slow down. Moving the cyclic laterally will make the helicopter turn. To put it simply – perhaps a bit too simply – you move the cyclic the way you want the helicopter to go.

Your stick movements need to be very small. It is very easy to move the cyclic too much, then realize what's happened and move it too far in the opposite direction. You quickly end up with what are known as 'pilot-induced oscillations'; that is, the helicopter starts swinging gently forward and back or from side to side, until your instructor takes over and sorts things out. Basically, you are over-correcting. But don't be alarmed; practice makes perfect, and you will soon learn the amount of movement that is required.

The next thing we need to look at is the design of cyclic you are using. In most helicopters, a stick rises vertically from the floor between the legs of each pilot. However, in the Robinson R22 and R44 that are commonly found in flying schools, there is a single cyclic control between the two pilots' seats, with a T-bar on the top, so that it can be used from either side. I've heard different reasons given for the Robinson design, but it's really not something we need to consider here. The important point is that the two designs work in exactly the same way, and it makes very little difference which one you have. You will possibly hear people say that one is better than the other, or that they don't like the Robinson design, or something similar, but both cyclic types are identical in all but looks, and it isn't something worth worrying about.

The Robinson-type T-bar cyclic control, used on the most popular training helicopter, the Robinson R22, and its bigger brother, the R44.

The conventional cyclic control used on most non-Robinson helicopters, in this case a Eurocopter Twin Squirrel.

Collective Control and Throttle

The collective, or lever, is on each pilot's left side, looking something like the handbrake in a car. It controls the height of the helicopter by altering the pitch of all the rotor blades collectively, hence the name. If you raise it, the helicopter climbs; if you lower it, the machine descends. Since more power is needed to climb, there is a twist-grip throttle on the end of the collective, so that it can be opened to climb and closed to descend. It works like a motorbike throttle, but if you're a biker, be careful, as it works in the opposite direction from what you'll be used to!

However, in most modern helicopters there is also an electronic governor which senses the position of the collective and automatically opens the throttle to the amount required, so you don't need to worry about throttle control at all; this is the case for the R22 and R44. But if you are learning on the Schweizer 300 or Enstrom 280 you will need to learn manual throttle control, as these aircraft are un-governed. It is not a big deal, as both these types have a mechanical correlator that adjusts the power required to a certain extent, so that the pilot just needs to keep an eye on it and tweak it a little now and then. And both these helicopters are probably a little easier to fly than the R22, so it's horses for courses and all that.

The collective lever, seen here at the bottom of photograph, sits by the pilot's left thigh.

Yaw Pedals

The last main control is the yaw pedals. Left pedal causes the helicopter's nose to turn left, while right pedal has the opposite effect. However, in forward flight the pedals are primarily used to keep the aircraft in balance; that is, flying straight rather than crabwise. You can tell whether or not you are flying in balance by looking at two strips of wool that are fitted to the front of every helicopter, and most of them also have a balance ball – a bit like a spirit level – among the cockpit instruments.

Yaw pedals.

Other Controls and Instruments

Your instructor may also mention other cockpit controls during this briefing, or during the flight. These may include such things as the carburettor heat switch if you are flying a carburetted helicopter, and any friction knobs, hydraulics and warning lights or horns. He might tell you about some of the cockpit instruments, or he may not, since the early flying exercises are best done using purely visual cues. He may tell you about some further effects of the controls, such as what happens when you lower the collective completely to enter auto-rotation. However, some of these things may be left for a later date, but if this is the case, make sure that you do learn about them eventually.

Practising the Controls

When it comes to the flying, you will handle each control separately – or you should. This may come as a surprise to anyone who has had a fairly long trial lesson, and who has maybe managed to cope with two or even three controls together. You might feel as though you're going backwards, and you want to do more. However, the aim of this exercise is to understand exactly what each control does, and this can only be properly achieved if each control is used alone. Later on you will start putting two controls together, and then all three. But it really isn't a good idea to hurry at this stage, or important things can get missed out.

You will learn to handle each control separately.

I found this out the hard way, because I wasn't taught things in this manner. My first few flying hours were done on a helicopter one-day introductory course, which mainly involved hands-on flying without much in the way of theory. This meant that by the time I decided definitely to do the formal PPL(H) course, I was fairly good at handling the controls, so my instructor let me use all three together. The result was that I never really did Exercise 4 in a formal fashion – until I came to do my Instructor's Rating. Believe me when I say that this is really, really not the best way to learn! Although I could fly helicopters quite adequately, and did so for years, my knowledge of how they worked was somewhat sketchy for quite a long time. I can see now that it would have been very useful for me to have learned more slowly in the early stages, even if it had meant apparently going over something I'd already done.

Another point to mention is that you should not be using the cockpit instruments during this lesson, or very little. It is important to learn to fly visually, and your instructor will show you how to find out if you are flying level, or turning, or climbing, or descending, by using a reference point in the cockpit and the natural horizon outside. It is extremely important to learn this from the start, so don't try to be clever and take a peek at the dials, as some people do. Although the instruments have their uses, you will fly better if you learn from the start to keep your eyes outside the cockpit, and once you start doing navigation and speaking on the radio, you simply won't have the capacity to monitor the instruments as well. Again, I learned this by experience. I wasn't taught to look outside the cockpit from the start, so I developed a habit of fixating on the instruments, and it was something I found rather hard to change. Learn from my mistakes, and don't do it!

Finally, don't be concerned if you find this first exercise quite difficult. There is a lot to learn, and it will be the first time you have tried to fly a helicopter accurately at the same time as monitoring what is happening. Helicopters are not easy machines to fly, and you may struggle initially, particularly with cyclic control. Have patience with yourself; it will come. If you end up doing Exercise 4 over two sessions, or even more, that's quite acceptable.

EXERCISE 5: ATTITUDE AND POWER CHANGES

In this exercise you will learn to use two controls together. It will probably be the first time you will have done this formally, although you may have had a go at using more than one control at a time on your trial lesson, for instance. The aim of this exercise will be to learn how to alter the attitude and power of the helicopter, in order to achieve a change in its speed and height.

Cyclic and Pedals

First, you will use the cyclic and pedals to alter the attitude of the helicopter, and this will also change its airspeed. Briefly, if you move the cyclic forward the aircraft will accelerate, and if you move it back again it will slow down. But you've already done this in Exercise 4, you might say. That is indeed the case, but in this exercise you will learn to increase and decrease speed more accurately, monitoring the speed using the Air Speed Indicator (ASI) in the cockpit, and eventually using specific airspeeds that you will try to reach and then hold as you continue flying. Again, particularly if you are flying the twitchy little R22, don't worry if you find this difficult – because it is difficult! No-one ever said that flying a helicopter was easy, so don't expect it to be. But the idea is primarily that you understand what it is that you are trying to do, and the accuracy will come with practice.

So where do the pedals come into all this, you might ask? You may have had it pointed out to you during Exercise 4 that when you push the cyclic forward the helicopter yaws left, and when you pull it back the machine yaws right. This is because the tail fin is more efficient at a higher airspeed; the effect isn't that obvious, so it may not have been mentioned yet, or you may have been so overloaded with new information that you didn't take it in. In this exercise it is important, however, as you are trying to keep the helicopter flying straight. Therefore as you move the cyclic forward and increase speed you will need to apply a little right pedal, and vice versa. Actually, if you simply try to keep flying in a straight line, you will probably find that you apply the correct amount of pedal fairly naturally.

Another important point in this part of the exercise is to note the phenomenon of 'flapback' (*see* page 28). When you move the cyclic forward, the rotor disc will tilt in that direction and the helicopter's speed will initially increase. However, owing to dissymmetry of lift, the disc will then flap back to its original position, and you will get no further increase in speed. Therefore you need to keep moving the cyclic forward in order to keep accelerating. It used to feel to me as though fairly constant forward pressure on the cyclic was required if the helicopter was not to slow down, but perhaps it would be more accurate to say that you can't actually move the cyclic forward and then relax; you have to keep working at it.

When you slow down you get flap-forward and a similar effect: the helicopter will stop decelerating – or so they say. Actually it's not very noticeable, so you probably won't need to think about it too much. In any case, while flapback occurs throughout the speed range of the helicopter, flap-forward only happens at low airspeeds, generally below 50kt or so.

You will use the cyclic and pedals together.

Collective and Pedals

The second half of Exercise 5 will involve using the collective and pedals together in order to climb and descend. If you are learning on a helicopter with an electronic governor, you will initially do this with the governor on, so you won't have to worry about throttle changes. If learning on another type, you may have to make small throttle adjustments as well. However, you will be shown that more power is needed to climb, and less power to descend, turning the governor off for a demonstration if necessary.

When you raise the collective, you will get an increase in manifold air pressure (MAP), which is a measure of the power of the engine. The helicopter will then start to climb. It will also yaw to the right, which will mean you need to apply left pedal in order to keep it flying straight. Then when you lower the collective to fly level, and eventually to descend, you will need to apply right pedal.

Perhaps the only real difficulty is actually understanding which control is responsible for which effect. This is probably due to the fact that most of us fly helicopters with governors, so we don't actually experience what happens when the throttle is opened and closed. I believed for ages that raising the collective caused the increase in MAP and power. However, it is actually the throttle increase that does this. The collective alters the pitch on the rotor blades, which gives the helicopter more lift, while the throttle controls the engine power, which needs to be increased for a climb to take place. If you increased pitch without increasing engine power, the rotor blades would slow down and eventually stop! So you need to use the collective and throttle together, but they do different things. It is perhaps a small point, and maybe obvious to some people. But it is very important, and worth always bearing in mind if you are to understand at all times what your helicopter is doing.

When flying with the governor off, the situation and what you need to do varies a lot, depending on what type of helicopter you are learning on. This is because almost all types have a mechanical correlator, which overcompensates in some aircraft at some MAP settings. This means that you may sometimes need to turn the throttle in what is apparently the 'wrong' direction. Don't worry about this too much now, as you will learn the relevant points for your particular type of helicopter; I just mention it because it can cause confusion, even among seasoned helicopter pilots. I remember, many years ago, being told that when you took off in an R22 without the governor, you needed to close the throttle or the rotor RPM would go too high; this is because the R22 correlator is one that overcompensates at low MAP settings. However, a very experienced army helicopter pilot, who had never encountered a helicopter with this sort of strange idiosyncrasy (as he perceived it) claimed that I must be wrong. If you raised the collective without opening the throttle, he insisted, the RPM would 'droop'. We were both right for our respective aircraft, and all this illustrates is that you need to know your own helicopter type and not make assumptions about others. Of course, it should be noted that in 'governed' helicopters the governor is never turned off during flight; you will only fly without it for lessons and demonstrations of emergencies.

I am digressing somewhat here. It should be emphasized that the second part of Exercise 5 is usually fairly simple to understand. It is maybe a little harder to do in practice, but most people find it easier than learning to handle the cyclic accurately. But overall, the exercise rarely takes a whole hour, so during this lesson you may also learn some other points, such as radio use, monitoring of the cockpit instruments and becoming aware of your location. You may also have warning horns and lights pointed out to you.

EXERCISE 6: LEVEL FLIGHT, CLIMBING, DESCENDING AND TURNS

Exercise 6 not only has a very long title, it is a rather a long exercise! You will finally be using all three helicopter controls together, in order to learn to fly a helicopter in any direction and at any height that you want. But you may not manage that all at once. Exercise 6 is often done in two or three sessions, so don't start thinking that you are a slow learner if this is the case for you.

During this exercise it is important to remember what each control is primarily used for. To recap: the cyclic controls attitude and airspeed, the collective is for height and power (the latter through the throttle) and the pedals keep the helicopter in balance. Some students can get very confused about this, because it isn't that obvious or cut and dried thanks to the 'secondary effects' of each control. For instance, pushing the cyclic forward will cause the helicopter to descend as well as speed up. Similarly, if you lower the collective, the helicopter might well speed up as well as descend, especially if you allow the nose to drop. And you can turn, though rather inefficiently, using the pedals. This is all true and very obvious to anyone who has done a little flying. But all the same, it is important to remember the main purpose of each control, particularly in the beginning, otherwise things can become very confused later on in your helicopter training.

Straight and Level Flight

Initially you will learn to fly straight and level at a given airspeed, usually 70kt. For this speed you will find that a certain power setting is required. If the helicopter starts climbing or descending, you will need to adjust either the attitude or the power. Since the cyclic is so sensitive, in practice it is usually the attitude that needs to be adjusted, but if that doesn't work, then you will need to alter the MAP setting using the collective.

Next will come speed increases and decreases. To increase speed, you will push the cyclic forward, as you did in the last exercise. However, in this case you don't want the helicopter to descend, so you will also raise the collective a little; then use whichever pedal is required in order to keep the helicopter flying in balance. For every airspeed, there is a power setting that will keep you flying level, and this can be shown on a graph. So, as you will see on the diagram overleaf, increased speed requires increased power, and when you decrease speed you decrease power. The only exception to this is at very low airspeeds, when you need to increase power again, and a very large amount of power is needed when your airspeed is nil, i.e. when hovering. Don't worry about this too much now, but you will need to bear it in mind later on. Reducing speed is done in the same way – bring the cyclic back, lower the collective a little and use the pedals for balance.

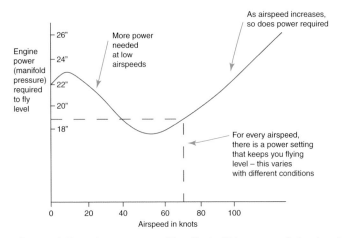

For every airspeed, there is a power setting that will keep you flying level.

For both of these manoeuvres it is important to keep looking outside as much as possible, and not 'chase' the airspeed on the instruments. There is a lag in all of the controls, so your input will not register on the dials until a second or two after you've made an adjustment; if you chase the controls you'll be doing it for ever. Therefore simply select the right picture in the windscreen, in the way your instructor will demonstrate to you, then hold that attitude, and adjust it later if necessary. There is a fine balance between sloppy flying that is not accurate enough, and trying too hard in the wrong way – and chasing the airspeed is a good example of the latter!

You will probably practise flying straight and level at a variety of airspeeds between 40–80kt or thereabouts. You can fly slower than that, but the controls can be difficult to handle at very low airspeeds, and you could also encounter other problems. And you don't want to go too fast in the early stages, as many training helicopters have a maximum permitted speed (VNE) of only around 90kt.

Climbing and Descending

To climb, you select the attitude for the airspeed you want – probably 60kt for this exercise. You then raise the collective and adjust the pedals; in this case you will need left pedal, as you will be making a large collective adjustment. Of course, you look out carefully and monitor your instruments to make sure all is well before you do this. To level off from the climb, move the cyclic forward to select the attitude for straight and level, then lower the collective and adjust using right pedal.

You will probably learn an acronym for the order in which to do both of these manoeuvres: APT, or attitude–power–trim. Of course, after a great deal of practice the whole thing will become a smoothly co-ordinated application of all the controls simultaneously, but this is the sequence that should be used when you are learning.

To descend, you look out first, then lower the collective, select the attitude and adjust the pedals. To level out from the descent you raise the collective, select the attitude and adjust the pedals again. In this case the acronym is PAT: power–attitude–trim. There is a good reason for this. If you selected a 60kt attitude for the descent first, the helicopter would start to climb. If you are flying a helicopter with a carburetted engine, you will need to apply full 'carb' heat before you lower the collective for the descent. Up until now you will have been monitoring the carburettor temperature and using a small amount of carb heat when necessary. However, the carb heat gauge is not accurate at low collective and power settings, and this is the situation in which carb icing is most likely. So for safety, whenever lowering the collective a large amount, you apply full carb heat first. Those flying helicopters with fuel-injected engines have one less thing to think about here.

To climb, you select the attitude for the airspeed you want. (Neil Harrison)

You will probably learn to climb and descend at a specific speed, which is about 60kt in the majority of training helicopters. There are sensible reasons for this. The first is that in most small helicopters this speed gives a rate of climb or descent around 500ft/min, which is a nice, steady pace and not too frightening for beginners. The second reason is that this is just slightly above the best rate of climb speed for most helicopters – the speed at which least power is required for straight and level flying. The trouble with using best rate of climb speed exactly would be that as soon as you either reduced or increased it at all, more power would be required, which could be very difficult for a student to handle. But if you fly a little faster – 60kt – then an increase in speed means more power is required, while a decrease means less power is required, which is much easier to cope with. Confused? Don't worry about it; you don't really need to understand it at this stage – I just thought you might be interested.

Why do you slow down to descend, you might ask? This is largely a safety issue. You could descend by maintaining the speed, lowering the collective and pushing the cyclic forward, and in fact this is the way commercial pilots often do it. But from a safety point of view it is a good idea to descend at a steady, not-too-fast pace, particularly when you are learning. However, there is a far more important reason for learning the manoeuvre in this way, and particularly for the order power–attitude–trim. It ensures that a phenomenon known as 'mast bumping' is prevented.

Mast bumping occurs when the helicopter's main rotor hub makes contact with and deforms the main rotor mast, causing the rotor to fall off the helicopter – definitely not a good idea! It only occurs in helicopters with two-bladed teetering rotor systems, but this includes the R22 and R44, which most people learn on, as well as the Bell 206 JetRanger, which many new pilots convert onto after gaining the PPL(H). There are a number of reasons for mast bumping, but the commonest is an abrupt movement forward of the cyclic, resulting in low 'g' (gravitational) force – in other words, weightlessness. This causes the rotor blades to flap far more than they were ever intended to, with possible catastrophic results. So at this stage of your training it is best to learn good habits and avoid any sudden forward movement of the cyclic when descending.

Another reason for descending at a lower airspeed is that you are gradually working up to learning to fly 'circuits' of the airfield, an important discipline for any pilot. When you fly these, you will be landing after your descent, so you will not want to be flying too fast during your approach to land. So the speeds used are chosen from a practical point of view, but they are not set in stone. Later on you will learn to fly, climb and descend at different airspeeds, so always be aware that it is quite possible and acceptable to do so ... but not yet.

Turns
Turning is usually done from a straight and level attitude, at 70kt. The first thing you need to do is look out well in all directions, particularly to the left if you are turning right, and vice versa. Why? Because you will be turning away from that direction, and there could be a faster aircraft there, which will then be behind you and might not have seen you. Helicopters have good visibility, but there are a few blind spots, so be careful to move your head as you look out, as it's very easy to miss other aircraft – as you've probably already discovered by now!

You should look out in all directions before turning.

The main problem when learning to turn is to try to stay flying level. Due to the side-by-side seating in helicopters, and the fact that you are probably using a reference point in the centre of the windscreen in order to stay level, it is easy to think you are level in a turn when in fact you are climbing or descending. This happens far more in steep turns, but it even occurs at the rate of turn – around 20 degrees – that you will be doing now. The way to adjust for this is to pick a reference point on the windscreen which is directly in front of you, and your instructor will show you how to do this.

In the turn, the cyclic controls the attitude and angle of bank, the collective controls the height and the pedals keep you in balance. You will need a little in-turn pedal to turn properly, so don't consider the pedals simply as footrests for this exercise, as so many students do in my experience!

Climbing and Descending Turns

Finally, you will put the manoeuvres you have just learned together in order to practise climbing and descending turns. You establish the climb or descent first, then roll on the angle of bank. In a climb, the rate of climb will decrease as you turn. In a descent, the rate of descent will increase as you turn. This is due to less lift being produced when the helicopter is turning, but I suggest that you don't worry too much about the details of this for now. If you have learned the climb, descent and turn properly, putting them together will not be too challenging; but as with everything else in helicopter flying, don't expect it to be a piece of cake initially.

Some students can become demoralized during Exercise 6, because so much new flying is involved. The exercise can seem to go on for ever, particularly if your training is broken up due to bad weather or other una-voidable factors causing cancellation of lessons. If this applies to you, bear in mind that this exercise includes practically all the manoeuvres you will need when going for a flight. When I was an instructor at a flying school at Sheffield City Airport, I used to demonstrate this to my students if they were getting depressed with the non-stop practice. I would take them on a little flight over the hills of the Peak District to visit Chatsworth House, a spectacular stately home a short distance away. We would start off flying straight and level; then I would point out that since there were hills ahead, perhaps climbing a little would be sensible. We would then fly level until we reached Chatsworth House, when I would suggest that they might like to descend in order to have a good look around, while remaining at a legal and safe altitude of course. I would then suggest that they circled around in order to be able to see the house and grounds better. Then we would reverse the procedure to go back to the airfield. This was an excellent way of not only showing them the practical uses of Exercise 6, but of demon-strating how much they had learned. It also gave them a good reason for learning to fly accurately with their eyes mainly outside the cockpit – for we wanted to be looking at the scenery, not the helicopter dials. I think most of my students found it to be an excellent learning experience – and a most enjoyable flight.

EXERCISE 7: BASIC AUTOROTATIONS

Exercise 7 heralds something of a change in the way the flying course has been progressing, for a number of reasons. Firstly, the whole lesson is based around a possible emergency: how to fly in the event of engine failure. This can sound very frightening to many people, so it should be emphasized that engine failure is extremely rare. Many helicopter pilots go through a whole lifetime of flying without needing to do an autorotation for real. So while some students shake in their shoes at the mere mention of autorotations, even practice ones, they really don't need to. This is merely an exercise. And it is quite safe to practise it, since you always have an engine there should it be required.

However, the myth that helicopters fall out of the sky if the engine stops is very widespread, which perhaps explains why it is even believed to a cer-tain extent by students – despite anything said to the contrary. Unfortunately, the myth has been perpetuated in books and films for years. Indeed, a book by a well-known thriller writer was spoiled for me by the description of a helicopter plunging out of control into the trees below after the engine had failed. It was such a pity – the story would have been much more convinc-ing, and far more exciting, had the pilot executed a perfect autorotation into a tiny clearing in the forest . . . as he probably would have done in real-ity. So remember, helicopters don't suddenly crash when the engine fails; this is definitely a myth.

The second big difference from your previous exercises is one that isn't mentioned very often. Indeed, I didn't realize what a dramatic change it represented until one of my students pointed it out to me. What is different is that up until now your instructor will probably have been telling you to be very gentle with the helicopter controls, and to make very small movements. In Exercise 7, however, that will change. You will need to lower the collective right down, as far as it will go, and do it quite quickly, almost aggressively. Some students are scared to do this, since it seems to go against everything they have so far been told about helicopter flying. If you feel that way, don't worry; it's OK to do this. You have to learn to use the controls appropriately, and that doesn't mean being gentle and subtle with them all the time.

The aim of Exercise 7 is to learn how to enter autorotation, control the helicopter as you descend, and recover to the climb. A little theory sometimes helps enormously here, both in terms of dispelling any lingering fear, and in understanding what is happening. Firstly, it is not the engine that ultimately keeps the helicopter flying. As explained in earlier sections, the air over the rotor blades produces lift, and it is this lift which enables the helicopter to stay in the air. Normally, however, we need the engine to turn the blades in order to produce that airflow and hence the lift required. So if the engine stops, something else is required to keep the blades turning. If you lower the collective quickly and start a descent, the resulting airflow coming from below will keeps the blades rotating, a little like a windmill or sycamore leaf. You will be able to monitor this visually on the cockpit instruments, since the needle on the rotor RPM gauge will stay 'in the green' – within the normal range – even when the throttle is closed. And that RPM means 'revolutions per minute' – in other words, the rotor blades are still turning at their normal rate.

So the helicopter can still fly. It is established in what is known as 'autorotation'. It will descend quite quickly, typically at around 1,700ft/min. But it will be coming down under control, and the pilot can choose where to go, decide to speed up or slow down, and turn into wind and select a safe landing site. At a height of about 40ft, the pilot will gently bring the cyclic back, causing the nose of the helicopter to rise a little above the horizontal. This manoeuvre is known as a 'flare'. The helicopter is then levelled at about 5–10ft, and at the last moment the collective is raised to cushion the landing. If this is done correctly, the helicopter will land gently, possibly with a short run-on as it touches the ground.

This sounds complicated – but you won't be doing all of it in this exercise. At this early stage of training you will be learning simply how to enter autorotation, control the aircraft in the descent, and recover to the climb; the rest will come later. The exercise will be started at a height of around 2,000ft or more, so that you can recover well above the ground and hopefully nothing will feel too rushed. For this reason, the autorotation exercise is often postponed until there is a day with suitable weather – a high cloud base is particularly important. So if you're apparently racing through the exercises, but have missed out Exercise 7, don't worry about it. It hasn't have been forgotten; you just probably haven't had a suitable day.

This lesson is usually done well away from the airfield. There are a number of checks to ensure that all is well, and the helicopter is turned into wind. If you are flying a helicopter with a carburretor, you apply full 'carb' heat. If your aircraft has a governor, it may or may not be turned off; it depends on your instructor's preference, and it doesn't make a lot of difference. Then your instructor will make a pre-arranged call, normally 'practice autorotation, go'. At this point you will lower the collective as far as possible. You will find that the nose tends to drop due to the airflow hitting the horizontal stabilizer, and the helicopter yaws left, as is normal when you lower the lever: you need to apply back pressure on the cyclic, and right pedal. It helps to have something specific to say to remind you to do this; I was taught to say 'down, right, back', at first, and later, by a different instructor, 'down on the lever, hold the attitude, right pedal'. You may be told to say something different, and the details don't really matter.

'Practice autorotation, go!'

Actually, if you look outside and keep the helicopter straight and level, just as you would when flying with an engine, you won't go far wrong. However, it does sometimes seem to be abnormally hard to do this when you know you're about to practise an autorotation! Fear has some strange effects, and if you find that you forget how to fly when starting this exercise, you're probably normal.

You are now established in autorotation. You need to look at the instrument panel and select an appropriate speed for your helicopter type, usually around 65kt. When all is well you close the throttle, although at this early stage your instructor may take care of that side of things. You might find now that the rotor RPM goes too high, which can damage the helicopter, so you will need to raise the collective slightly, or 'pinch an inch' as it is often put. There will be a warning light and/or horn to tell you if you overdo it and slow down the rotor blades by raising the collective too much. But don't overreact to this horn; it is quite easy to get your RPM back again. Also, there is a lag between operating the lever and the RPM registering on the dial, so as I've said before, don't 'chase' the instruments.

At around 500–1,000ft, you will start the recovery. This is done by opening the throttle, raising the collective and establishing a normal climb. This all needs to be done firmly but gently. Don't open the throttle so enthusiastically that you overspeed the rotors, as one of my students nearly did once! Since the collective will be almost on the floor of the helicopter, it will need to be raised by a large amount, with a corresponding input of left pedal; you will also need some forward pressure on the cyclic. But again, don't go mad with all this; simply establish the correct attitude and power for the climb. The first time you do this exercise your instructor may take care of the recovery since you are not accustomed to the somewhat aggressive moves required, but later on it will be something that you can do.

After a little autorotation practice, you will probably do a few manoeuvres while descending, such as turns. You will find that the rotor RPM will increase in a turn and decrease as you roll out of the turn, meaning that small collective adjustments will be required. Again, don't worry if you have trouble with doing this at this stage of your helicopter training. You might also look at the effect of airspeed changes and flaring the helicopter, or these might be left for a later exercise.

One of the problems with this particular exercise is that the pace at which it is done cannot be altered to any great extent. By that, I mean that once the collective is lowered, things cannot be slowed down: if the autorotation is started at 2,500ft and the rate of descent is a typical 1,700ft/min, there is about one minute to do everything required before recovery has to commence. The result is that this exercise can feel rather rushed for those of us who are not the fastest learners in the history of rotary aviation. If you are one of those, join a fairly large club! But a few little hints may help to some extent.

First, which way should you move the collective to adjust the rotor RPM? This is something with which I always had trouble, as there just didn't seem to be time to work it out. So a useful tip is to follow the RPM needle: if the needle is too high, raise the collective a little; if too low, push it down. Second, make a conscious effort to look outside most of the time, not at the instruments. That way you will quite naturally make the correct movements of the controls. Trust yourself! Next, make a real effort to take deep breaths. It sounds obvious, but if you are tense you forget to breathe, and this doesn't help when it comes to autorotation practice, or flying in general. Finally, to repeat myself, remember that you do have an engine there if it is needed. If everything goes pear-shaped, you can open the throttle and fly normally. So, as I've said several times already, don't worry.

EXERCISE 8: HOVERING

Hovering is difficult, at least to begin with, and frequently for quite a long time afterwards. Everyone who has ever flown a helicopter – or tried to – knows this. It is unlike practically anything else in or outside of rotary aviation, it takes time to learn, and when you start it can seem absolutely impossible.

For this reason, Exercise 8 is rarely done as a completely separate exercise. At many flying schools – although not all – hovering is taught right from the beginning of the course, in short sessions of around 10 minutes at the end of every lesson. This is the way I have always done it, both when I was a student and as an instructor, so long as the weather and other practical factors are on our side. The main reason is that learning to hover is extremely tiring, and the beginner simply would not be able to manage an hour of it. Furthermore, the only way to learn to hover effectively is to relax while you are doing it, and you can't do that when you start to get tired, grit your teeth in determination and vow to carry on no matter what – this may be a laudable attitude, but it simply doesn't work. So if hovering is actually taught as a separate lesson it tends to be in half-hour sessions with a break in between. Often students will start off with 10-minute sessions at the end of other exercises, working up to these longer periods as their skill increases, and that does seem to work well. Or you may find you move on to later exercises, coming back to hovering in order to improve your skill.

Hovering may be really hard, but it is also tremendous fun. I'm not the only person to have become totally hooked on rotary flying the first time I managed to hover with all three controls. It was only for 35 seconds – my instructor was counting. But that was it – I knew I just had to carry on. I had been a fixed-wing pilot and had gone for a rotary trial lesson just for something different to do, with no intention of continuing. But that half-minute or so changed my life, and I've never regretted it.

Hovering is commonly described as being like trying to pat your head and rub your stomach at the same time. While this analogy is vastly over-used, it is not inaccurate. The helicopter has three highly sensitive controls, all of which operate differently and all of which affect each other. To further complicate matters, there is a lag between operating each control and the helicopter responding. And to really confuse the new student, there is a different amount of lag for each control.

Hovering is great fun. (Neil Harrison)

So let us look at what this means in practice when you start learning to hover. We know that the collective controls the helicopter's height by altering the pitch of the main rotor blades, while the yaw pedals control the pitch of the tail rotor blades. So if you raise the collective, the helicopter will climb, but it will also yaw to the right, so you will need to apply left pedal to keep the aircraft straight. Therefore, you might think, if you're hovering and feel the helicopter sinking, you raise the collective and put in a bit of left pedal. But there's a large amount of lag in the collective, so you raise it but you don't seem to be climbing. Thinking you haven't done enough, you raise the collective more, remembering to put in lots of left pedal as you do so. Suddenly the helicopter positively shoots into the air. In mild panic, you lower the collective, but nothing seems to happen, so you lower it still further. And all of a sudden you're heading full speed for the ground, and yawing violently left – because in your haste you forgot that your large movement of the collective meant that you would need a similar amount of pedal.

Meanwhile you're also trying to handle the cyclic. As you'll already know, this is by far the most sensitive of the three controls, and this is particularly the case in the hover. So while you're sorting out your collective and pedals, the helicopter is probably moving rapidly ... in some direction or another. In fact, the machine will now probably be oscillating wildly, performing amazing low-level gyrations, and completely out of control. Very soon, your instructor will utter the magic words 'I have control'. And somehow, quite miraculously, the errant machine will be quickly brought to a rock-steady hover. You can now try the same thing again.

This is why you will learn to operate one control at a time when you start hovering. When you become proficient at this you will move on to two controls together, then all three. But this could take several sessions. In fact, the amount of time people take to learn to hover varies tremendously, but for many it can be an incredibly frustrating experience. I have known students who even considered giving up the whole course, as they were having such a hard time learning to hover. Some people try to find a short-cut; a common method is to try to centralize all the controls, to find some mid-point at which the helicopter will maintain a steady hover and not move. After all, this is what seems to be happening when the instructor takes over – he or she hardly seems to be moving the controls at all. But this just doesn't work, because the helicopter is 'dynamically unstable'. That means that it won't simply stay in one position with no input from the pilot. If you don't move the cyclic at all, the helicopter gets into some rather interesting forward and backward oscillations, which gradually increase. Try it some time – but not too close to the ground, and preferably with an instructor on board.

So how can you learn to hover more easily? What can be done to make this a less painful process? Well, ultimately, nothing! It all comes down to practice. Hovering is a bit like learning to ride a bike – it seems impossible until you can do it, and then you wonder what on earth was so difficult. The fact is that you are making new pathways from your hands and feet to your brain, as it were, and this just takes time. It is the way that any new skill is learned, and hovering is really no different from learning to drive a car, or ride a horse, or play football, or learn a martial art. In one sense, an instructor cannot 'teach' you to hover – he or she can merely prevent you from killing yourself while you learn.

However, there are a few techniques to make it easier and quicker. The first and most important one is to relax. It is true that this is very hard to do when you are learning to hover, but it works, and its importance cannot be over-emphasized. A relaxed attitude somehow makes it easier for those new hand/foot-to-brain pathways to develop. For this reason the students who learn to hover most quickly are often the ones who don't try too hard. Of course, you have to put in a certain amount of effort, but grim determination, with all its accompanying frustration and tension, just gets in the way. Those who simply enjoy the crazy oscillations of early hovering practice, and accept that the learning process takes time, often pick up hovering most quickly.

Second, you need to know what to do with your eyes – in other words, where to look. It is tempting to stare at the ground, as you're so frighteningly close to it, but this doesn't work. There are various theories, but picking a reference point in the distance, and then a feature about 20–30ft away, seems to work best. That way, you will notice if your chosen points move in relation to each other, and thereby pick up on small deviations and movements of the helicopter. And it's far, far easier to make small corrections than large ones, as any adjustment of one control will necessitate large movements of the other controls too, and that's when things usually start to go haywire. Don't worry; you will see the ground with your peripheral vision anyway. You don't need to consciously look at it, and if you do, you'll tend to fly into it.

Most people feel as though they need an area about the size of a football field when they first start learning to hover. Then gradually you manage in a smaller area. Eventually there will come that magic moment when – you've got it; you can hover! But then you realize that, as with many things in aviation, there is a lot more to the process than you first thought.

Wind is the first thing that may cause the goalposts to move as far as your hovering practice is concerned. If you started flying helicopters in the summer, you may have been lucky enough to learn to hover in nil-wind conditions. But when the wind picks up in autumn, you will realize that this has become a whole new ball game. Hovering into wind will present you with little difficulty by now. But if you turn out of wind, you'll probably find that the helicopter suddenly shoots off downwind. You'll find that you need to move the cyclic towards the wind direction. And if you turn downwind, the wind now blows on alternate sides of the tail, causing the helicopter to yaw erratically, and you need to be very quick on the pedals to keep it under control. When the wind is from the left, the tail rotor is affected, and you need to react even faster with your use of the pedals.

Wind will also affect a closely related skill, hover-taxying, which is not a separate exercise but is usually included here. This is merely hovering while moving slightly forward, and once students have mastered the hover it generally isn't too difficult. Indeed, in light winds, some people find it easier to hover while moving slightly forward rather than keeping still over one spot. But in a strong-ish wind, hover-taxying can become really difficult for the low-hours pilot, and you will probably need to be aware of this for quite a long time, even after you are fairly confident about hovering.

But for now, be aware that it is normal to find hovering difficult and hang on in there. Soon you will start to find that it is tremendously enjoyable. Why? Because if you like hands-on flying, this is about as hands-on as it gets. When you can do it, you feel like you've strapped on the helicopter almost as an extension of yourself. You can move in any direction, and take off and land almost anywhere – with lots of interesting manoeuvres in between, and constant on-going challenges. You can do practically anything, limited only by your own skill.

As part of this exercise you will learn to deal with engine failure in the hover. Your instructor will close the throttle, and you will learn to land safely. The most important thing is to hold the collective position while keeping the helicopter straight with the cyclic and pedals, then raise the collective slightly as the helicopter settles onto the ground. It's easier than it sounds!

EXERCISE 9: TAKE-OFFS AND LANDINGS

Take-offs and landings follow on directly from hovering, and you will probably start to learn them as soon as you can manage a steady hover. Landings are easier than take-offs for most people, so they are usually taught first.

Landings

Many students achieve their first landing without even realizing they are going to do it; this is certainly how I was taught it. My instructor simply told me to hover a little lower, then lower, then lower still: finally the helicopter touched the ground. The instructor simply pushed the collective right down, then turned to me with a pleased expression on his face and told me 'You've just done your first landing.' It was a good teaching method, as it got me over the student's common fear of being close to the ground. It was also a great confidence booster. So I teach landings this way too, and so do many other instructors . . . and now I've given the game away!

Hover lower and lower until the helicopter touches the ground. (Neil Harrison)

Whatever teaching technique is used in your case, to achieve a good landing you need to start with a steady hover. Relax, look well ahead, and hover lower and lower. It is important to make sure there is no sideways or backwards movement of the helicopter before the skids make contact with the ground, or you could catch a skid and turn the helicopter over. However, a little forward movement is acceptable, and some people find this easier than trying to maintain a rock-steady hover. But whatever technique you are using, as soon as the skids touch the ground, lower the lever decisively and land; you don't want to be messing around at that point. And that's about all there is to it!

There are, however, a few other things to know concerning landings. First, one skid will touch the ground first, and unless you are learning on a French or Russian helicopter, this is likely to be the left skid. You may or may not have realized by now that most helicopters – British and American ones anyway – hover left skid low. This is due to an aerodynamic effect caused by the presence of the tail rotor and its reaction with the main rotor. If you want further details, look up 'Tail Rotor Drift' and 'Tail Rotor Roll' in a textbook. But from a practical point of view, just be aware that this will happen and that it isn't that you're doing anything wrong; just carry on with the landing.

The next important point is that as you approach the ground, you may find that your steady hover suddenly changes. You're gradually lowering the collective, but the helicopter doesn't seem to want to go any lower; instead, it slides and skates over an invisible barrier. You're not going crazy; this is indeed just what is happening. The air that is drawn down through the rotors, known as the 'induced flow', usually dissipates, but as the helicopter gets close to the ground it cannot do this. Therefore the air gathers beneath the skids, and the resulting 'ground cushion' can literally hold the helicopter away from the ground. The strength of this ground cushion depends on the type of surface on which you are landing, and it's much more noticeable on a hard surface than on grass. For this reason, you'll probably learn to land on grass initially, and then have quite a shock when you come to land on asphalt or concrete. But whatever the surface, when you encounter this 'ground effect' simply keep going; carry on lowering the lever gently but firmly, not allowing the helicopter to get away from you. Like everything else in rotary aviation, you'll find that it gets easier with practice.

The final effect I need to mention is 'ground resonance'. This is a vibration of the helicopter, which occurs when it is close to or actually on the ground. It usually starts with a gentle rocking for no apparent reason, but if no correcting action is taken, the vibration will increase in amplitude until severe damage occurs to the helicopter.

Ground resonance is known to be uncommon in the R22, and I've never actually encountered it in any of the other helicopters I've flown. It can be caused by a number of factors, but you are fairly unlikely to have it happen. However, you do need to be aware of its possibility. If ground resonance ever does happen when you're flying, lift off and get away from the ground if at all possible. If that can't be done, you need to lower the collective fully, reduce power and apply the rotor brake. This is a brake that is applied to the rotors to slow them down, usually by pulling a cord or lever in the cockpit. Not all helicopters have them, but if yours does, you will probably have used it by now.

Take-Offs

You will probably find taking off more difficult than landing. Initially it doesn't sound too hard: you centralize the cyclic, then raise the collective slowly until the helicopter is light on the skids. At this point you adjust the cyclic position so that the aircraft is completely vertical, then you slowly raise the collective to lift the helicopter off the ground, keeping straight with the pedals, and adjusting the cyclic further if necessary.

The main problem is the complete and absolute necessity of taking off vertically, with no sideways movement whatsoever. The reason you simply must get this right, every time, is the possibility of an aerodynamic phenomenon known as 'dynamic rollover', which is important enough to go into in some detail even in this introductory text. Every so often an accident is reported involving a helicopter that crashed before it had even taken off. The pilot started up the machine, did all the necessary checks and prepared to depart, and then began to lift the helicopter into a hover as usual. But the helicopter didn't raise itself into a hover; instead, it suddenly and for no apparent reason turned over onto its side. And, since the rotors were running, it then proceeded to rather expensively thrash itself to bits. How could this happen?

If you look carefully at a helicopter, it would seem that it would be quite difficult to turn it over, so long as you had some idea of how to fly it. Helicopters sitting on the ground appear to be quite stable: their skids are normally spaced fairly far apart, forming a wide and apparently stable base. Surely, you would think, the only way to turn such a helicopter over on take-off would be to lift off at such an angle that the centre of gravity fell outside of the skids. And wouldn't this involve some pretty serious mishandling?

You would be quite correct in your thinking, if the displacement of the helicopter's centre of gravity were the only factor to be considered. If the helicopter were sitting on the ground without its engine turning this would indeed be the case; it could only overturn if it were on a very steep slope – a situation known as static rollover. But additional factors are involved in dynamic rollover. Power is being applied, and this means that the whole situation becomes completely different.

When you raise the collective to lift the helicopter off the ground, the total rotor thrust acts vertically, but it also has a horizontal component, which acts about the point of ground contact of the skids. Normally this is not a problem, as this component is very small and is opposed by the weight of the helicopter. But if one skid lifts off the ground first, the remaining skid now acts as a pivot point about which the horizontal component acts. This component increases as more power is applied and/or the angle of bank becomes steeper, causing the helicopter to tend to roll about the skid which is in contact with the ground, to a greater and greater extent. Beyond a certain critical angle it is impossible to stop the helicopter entering dynamic rollover and turning over. The angle of bank at which this can happen is fairly small, often less than 10 degrees, and far, far less than that required for static rollover.

The phenomenon of dynamic rollover is the reason why take-offs in a helicopter must be undertaken with such care, and why your instructor won't let you even attempt them until you've got your hovering just right. You really need to do it in two stages: raise the collective very slowly until the helicopter is light on the skids, then STOP! Now position the cyclic to ensure that your take-off will be precisely vertical, before raising the collective further. If you realize that the helicopter is not lifting off absolutely vertically, don't raise the collective further to get away from the ground, which is many people's instinctive reaction. This would increase the horizontal component of TRT, making the situation worse. The only thing to do is to lower the collective, get back on the ground, and then try again.

Taking off should be done with great care.

The necessity for perfect take-offs held me up for a while during my early helicopter training; I really struggled with this exercise. If this is the case with you, don't despair. As with all the rest of the course, practice makes perfect, and in time it will come.

EXERCISE 10: TRANSITIONS

Up until now you will have been flying the helicopter in two entirely different modes of flight: upper air work at speeds above 40kt, and hovering or hover-taxying close to the ground. Now the time has come to learn about moving from one to the other, and the term 'transition' refers to all flight from and to the hover.

The Hover to Forward Flight
Transitioning from the hover to forward flight is fairly easy to do, but much harder to understand. There are several quite complex aerodynamic effects that occur, and it helps if you understand a little about these.

You start in a steady hover, check that the area behind you is clear, then move the cyclic forward. This causes the helicopter to move forward and accelerate, but these are not the only things that happen. Remember, when a helicopter is hovering, air is being drawn down through the rotor system and collecting beneath the aircraft, forming a so-called 'ground cushion'. This cushion of air means that slightly less power is needed to hover close to the ground than would otherwise be the case. However, when the helicopter is moved forward from the hover, it literally falls off the cushion and starts to sink, and it is therefore necessary to raise the collective a little to maintain height.

This is what I and many other helicopter students learned initially as the explanation for this loss of height, and it make sense. However, not everyone agrees with this way of looking at the situation. While it is indeed true that as you move the cyclic forward the helicopter starts to sink, many authorities say the reason for this is that the lift vector (TRT) now has a horizontal component. In other words, the power that was being used simply to counteract the weight of the helicopter now has to not only do that, but also move the helicopter forward, so you need more power. This is perhaps a more generally accepted reason, but some experts mention both effects, and the real reason is possibly a combination of the two phenomena.

The next thing that happens as the aircraft moves forward is that it begins to roll to the right, so that a little left cyclic is required. This is due to different amounts of lift being produced at different points along the rotor blades at very low airspeeds, although the exact theoretical reason is somewhat more complicated than this. In practice this 'inflow roll' is a very small effect, if it occurs at all. Until I became an instructor I was never aware of having experienced it, and I still find it quite hard to demonstrate it to students, since in the Robinson R22 at least, you have to accelerate very, very slowly for it to happen at all. The reason for that is partly that other aerodynamic effects soon begin to take over.

The next effect – and this one is really noticeable – is the 'flapback' that was discussed in Chapter 1. To recap: when the cyclic is moved forward, the 'rotor disc' (the hypothetical disc the rotors make when they are rotating) tilts forward and down, and this is what causes the helicopter to move forward. However, owing to dissymmetry of lift the disc tends to try to flap back to its original position. This means that although a forward movement of the cyclic initially causes the helicopter to speed up, that acceleration will very quickly cease unless the pilot continues to hold the cyclic forward. So constant forward pressure on the cyclic is required as you continue the transition.

The next aerodynamic effect that happens is called 'translational lift'. At around 12–15kt of airspeed, some of the air that is being sucked down into the rotor system is blown away horizontally, and this means that more air is available to help the helicopter climb. In other words, it is free lift, and this is one of the few occasions when you get something for nothing. You will definitely notice this one, for the helicopter will really try to climb unless you prevent it doing so. However, at this point in the transition we don't want the helicopter to climb. Therefore when translational lift occurs, you need to push the cyclic firmly forward to convert lift energy into forward airspeed, while keeping close to the ground. At around 45kt, which is a safe flying speed, you ease back on the cyclic and allow the helicopter to climb, then push the cyclic forward a little to select the usual climb speed of 60kt. At this point the helicopter will tend to yaw left due to the fact that the tail fin is more efficient at higher airspeeds; it will also tend to roll left. Therefore both right cyclic and right pedal will be required. That is the transition completed, and the helicopter is now in forward flight.

Transitioning to forward flight is quite easy, but hard to understand. (Neil Harrison)

Reading this for the first time, or after sitting through a briefing on the subject, you might well think that the transition from the hover to forward flight requires incredibly fast reactions and the ability to do several things at the same time. Indeed, when I first learned all this I wondered how you could possibly do it all in practice. However, as I said at the beginning of the section, this manoeuvre is one that is actually far more difficult to describe than to do. In practice, what you need to do is bring the helicopter to a hover, look well ahead, and then move the cyclic forward. You then adjust all the controls as much or as little as is required until the helicopter is in forward flight. It is possible to do this without much real knowledge of the aerodynamic factors involved; you will tend by now to do the correct things naturally in order to keep the helicopter moving in the right direction. In fact, until I became an instructor I had only a vague idea of how all this worked ... and I suspect I was in good company! In practice, transitions from the hover to forward flight are quite easy, and most students pick them up quickly.

Why do we transition to forward flight in this way? After all, helicopters can climb vertically, so why not just lift the collective and keep climbing until you get to the height you want to be at, then move the cyclic forward to pick up speed? Indeed, you can depart in this manner, but normally helicopters accelerate close to the ground if at all possible, and only take off vertically or nearly so if they absolutely have to, in order to avoid trees or other obstacles. There is a good reason for this. If the engine were to fail at any point, you want to be able to put the helicopter into autorotation and land safely. This would be very difficult if the helicopter were to be high and slow, so you accelerate to a safe flying speed close to the ground, and then allow the helicopter to climb. It would also be difficult if the helicopter were moving very fast close to the ground. A graph can be plotted to show the heights and speeds at which safe recovery from engine failure would be unlikely, and the transition to forward flight is deliberately designed to stay out of this 'avoid curve', or as the Americans more graphically call it, the 'dead man's curve'. So we do the transition to forward flight in this way primarily for safety.

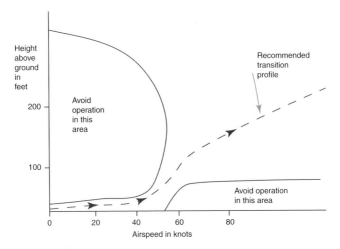

Stay out of the 'avoid curve'.

Forward Flight to the Hover

The transition from forward flight to the hover is the converse of the previous transition in that it is quite easy to explain, but many students find it much harder to do. At around 500ft above the ground you select a landing point. You then keep that point at a specific position on the windscreen, raising or lowering the collective as required in order to maintain a constant angle of approach. Meanwhile, you slow down gradually, using the cyclic. The deceleration is done progressively, from around 300ft above the ground, by noting the apparent groundspeed, and keeping that the same as you descend. In practice this produces a gradual slowing down of the aircraft. If you bear in mind that speed over the ground is far less noticeable at altitude, you'll understand how that works. If you keep the speed at what appears to be a steady walking pace, you'll get it about right. Then at around 100ft you simply look ahead and come gradually forward and down to normal hover height.

Come gradually forward and down to a hover. (Neil Harrison)

You will probably practise this manoeuvre with one control at a time initially. You will first use the collective to learn to make a steady approach by keeping your landing point at the same position on the windscreen; then you will start to use the cyclic to adjust the speed. The last part of the transition is often what people find difficult in the beginning. As you decelerate, more power is required, since translational lift is lost. And you will need a lot more power as you come to a hover. Therefore you need to be quite quick with the collective, and this also means that a fair amount of pedal work is required.

Because of this, students often manage fine until about the last 100ft, then everything starts to go wrong. If this occurs, if you are too high or too low, or the speed is wrong, it is best to do a 'go-around': push the cyclic forward, pull up on the collective, climb to a safe height and start again. It is rarely a good idea to try to recover at this point, as a high rate of descent with very low airspeed can be dangerous. This is one of the very few situations in which a helicopter can literally fall out of the sky. The phenomenon, known as 'vortex ring', will be explained in detail in the next chapter as part of the discussion of Exercise 15. For now, just bear in mind that you should not be descending at more than 300ft/min if your airspeed is less than 30kt. Those figures give you a bit of leeway, but if you remember them then it ensures that you are safe. If you need to descend faster than that at low airspeed, it is better to do a go-around; likewise if you are too low and fast, and the helicopter might get out of control.

The transition exercise covers a great deal, so you may well need two sessions or more to master it completely. As I've said before with respect to other exercises, don't worry if this turns out to be the case.

EXERCISE 11: CIRCUITS

This exercise brings together everything you have been learning up until now: take-off, hover and hover-taxi, transition, climb, turn, level off, descend, transition to hover, and finally land. It also involves you in flying in a specific pattern around the airfield, doing a number of aircraft checks at various points, keeping a good look-out at all times, and making several radio calls when and where required. Small wonder, then, that many students find their early circuit sessions stressful and extremely hard work. They feel that there just seems to be far too much to do, and the instructor seems to be expecting the impossible. Everything is happening too fast, and they wonder if they'll ever be able to manage it.

The circuits exercise brings everything together.

If this is the case with you, don't be surprised. For despite the fact that you have learned the relevant flying exercises, putting them all together can involve quite a high workload, especially in the beginning. Ideally you will have spent long enough on each separate exercise that you are quite comfortable with it, for this will mean that you now have time to concentrate on the newer aspects of circuit flying. However, this is not the case for every student. Some instructors prefer not to spend too long on Exercise 6, as too much repetition at an early stage can become disheartening for some students. So they move on, and plan to spend more time teaching the basics in the circuit. Other instructors – and I am one of those – feel that the basics of flying are better learned away from the airfield and the pressures of being near other traffic, however long that takes.

This means that students start Exercise 11 with varying degrees of experience and skill. Indeed, I have known of some students who reached this point but were then taken away from the airfield by their instructors after a circuit session or two, for more basic practice in climbing, descending and other such basics. Whichever of these varying scenarios applies to you, it really doesn't matter very much. It comes down mainly to different teaching techniques. If you find yourself being taken away from the airfield to re-do Exercise 6, this is not a retrograde step. You have not failed, or got worse, or any similar possibilities which might go through your head. Your instructor simply thinks that you might learn better away from a busy airfield, and he or she is probably right.

So what does Exercise 11 actually involve? The details depend on the specific airfield, but most points are very similar. You will make the relevant radio call, then take off and hover-taxi to your point of departure. Here you will do your pre-take-off checks, and the very last thing you will do before transitioning away is to look behind you. There may be landing traffic, and the last thing you want to do is transition away in front of it. You will then climb to circuit height, which is different at each airfield, making a climbing turn at the relevant point on to the crosswind leg, and of course looking out before you do so. You will level off at circuit height and make a turn onto the downwind leg; these may be done in the reverse order, depending on when you reach circuit height. Halfway along the downwind leg you make a call on the radio to report your position; then do various checks to ensure everything is safe for landing. At the appropriate position you turn on to base leg; then start a descent. The details after this may vary slightly depending on the airfield and your instructor, but you will probably level off at 500ft, do a level turn on to final, and then make a radio call. You then begin a transition to the hover exactly as you have been taught. If the approach doesn't look good, you do a go-around; otherwise you land.

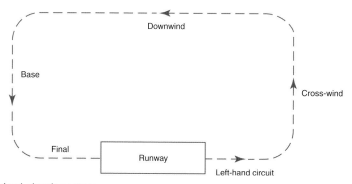

A standard circuit pattern.

This all sounds relatively straightforward, and indeed it is, for you have done it all before. Any difficulties are usually caused by the fact that everything has to be done quite quickly, and at a specific point or time. You also need to fly accurately and, as explained above, it helps if you've had enough practice before starting on circuits to be able to do this without too much effort. In addition you need to know where you are going, and the circuit route will of course be completely new to you in the beginning. However, your instructor will show you where to go – where and when to turn, how to recognize the important points in the circuit, etc – but it will probably take a little while for you to feel comfortable with it. Following the circuit pattern will also involve dealing with drift caused by the wind and coping with other weather conditions. Furthermore, you may need to deal with instructions from ATC and/or managing your own traffic avoidance, depending on the type of airfield at which you are flying. Although this won't be completely new to you at this stage, you probably won't have spent as much time close to other aircraft as you now will in the circuit. This will all add substantially to your workload, particularly if you are learning to fly at a busy airfield.

So don't beat yourself up if you find this exercise hard. The main thing is to keep your priorities in mind. In particular, it is important not to get too bogged down with speeds and heights – although they are important – but to remember what it is that you are actually doing. The purpose of circuits is to enable all airfield traffic to be flying in the same pattern around the field, primarily for safely. So situational awareness, keeping a good lookout and being aware of other traffic are all more important than whether your speed and altitude are 'on the numbers' – though obviously you don't want to be 300ft too high, particularly at airfields that have helicopter circuits below the fixed-wing ones!

The circuit exercise actually teaches you how to be a pilot: it develops captaincy, airmanship and decision-making skills as well as pure flying ones. Despite having a definite path to follow in the circuit, you need to be flexible and able to change your route and speed if necessary. Therefore, if there is another helicopter in front of you, it's fine and sensible to make your circuit a little larger or to slow down a bit. Your instructor should be very happy if you do that before he tells you to, but if he isn't, learn from what he says. Similarly, if it's not safe for you to turn onto base leg due to other traffic, then you can extend downwind, so that you turn behind the other aircraft. If you feel unsafe attempting to land, for any reason, simply perform a go-around and do it all again.

Different airfields have different procedures, but you may find yourself on the same runway as the fixed-wing traffic, or parallel to them, perhaps on a grass runway. There may be rules as to whether or not you are allowed to land when a fixed-wing aircraft is landing next to you. These vary from airfield to airfield, and it is important that you learn them and follow them. But to repeat, the most important thing is to fly safely.

Talking of safely, this exercise should also include a session on emergencies in the circuit. Again, this will all be stuff you have done before – how to land should the engine fail at any point, and what to do in the event of other emergencies such as radio failure, an electrical malfunction, or governor failure. For most emergencies other than an engine failure or engine fire you can simply make a radio call, complete your circuit and land. In the event of engine failure you need to enter autorotation, landing into wind as you have been taught – except for engine failure in the hover, but you should by now know how to deal with this.

Now, if you read this and think that you wouldn't feel completely happy doing an autorotation from 300ft after take-off, don't worry: neither would anyone else, given the choice! The point is that you do know how to do it and would stand a good chance of landing safely – and it is very, very unlikely to actually happen. However, the circuit exercise is the last lesson before going solo, so you do need to know how to deal with anything and everything that might come up, at least in theory.

Some students wonder, even at this stage, why the circuit exercise exists at all. After all, helicopters can take off and land almost anywhere, and they don't really need runways. Why are we emphasizing what is essentially a fixed-wing procedure? Well, most of us do have to operate at airfields, at least for part of the time, so we need to be able to fit into their way of doing things. But in addition to this, flying a circuit pattern is a useful way of preparing to land almost anywhere, as you will find out when you come on to later exercises. So trust the syllabus and your instructor, for this exercise does indeed have a use.

As already stated, you may find yourself spending quite a while doing circuits, but it really doesn't matter. For after that, if all goes well and there is no particular need to change the order of the exercises, will come your first solo flight!

EXERCISE 12: FIRST SOLO

First solo! For many students this is their goal, something they have been looking forward to from the first moment they sat in an aircraft. It is an aim, a dream, something which they expect to be wonderful and life-changing. But there is a little more to it than that.

For many students, going solo is a dream. (Neil Harrison)

There are a number of pre-requisites for your first solo flight, apart from reaching the required flying standard. To start with, it is a legal requirement that you have a valid medical certificate. For most people this is little more than a formality. However, I have known of students who turned out to have some unforeseen medical problem, and even if it is only something minor, such things can take a while to sort out. I mentioned this briefly in the first section of the book, so hopefully you obtained your medical early on and have nothing to worry about. But if not, now is the time to get it. But if there are any problems, don't worry, as it is perfectly possible – though perhaps disappointing – to continue with later exercises before doing your first solo.

There are a few other things you need to do before your first solo flight. You should have had an engine-off landing to the ground demonstrated to you, if you haven't tried one yourself – officially that exercise comes later in the course, but some students do attempt them earlier on. You may well have had 'vortex ring state' shown to you, and this is quite a good idea. You will have discussed and/or had demonstrated a number of other circuit emergencies. And you will need to do some paperwork, which varies slightly at different flying schools, but generally involves having read and signed the Flying Order Book and passed the Air Law ground exam. Note that while having a valid medical certificate is a legal requirement, having passed Air Law is not; however, most schools do require it, and it is definitely a good idea.

After that? Well, the weather needs to be suitable, and most schools have limits for first solo flights, often wind strength 10–15kt, visibility 5km and cloud base 1,000ft, although these do vary from one place to another. And of course the student needs to have reached the required standard, in terms of mental attitude and confidence as well as flying ability.

In fact, students vary greatly in these two attributes. Some people are champing at the bit, desperate to 'go solo' long before they are really ready for it. Others are more nervous and would rather keep the instructor with them a little longer. A few students have even been known to refuse to do their first solo flight when asked to. While some instructors will try to force people like that to do the exercise if they feel they are ready for it, I personally feel it is better to wait for confidence to grow in such circumstances. However, it is best to trust your instructor – if he or she says you are ready you almost certainly are; if he says you aren't, it's better to wait. After all, what's the rush? As mentioned earlier, there is a bit of a mystique that has grown up around first solo, with people perceiving it as a life-changing event. But to be realistic, it really doesn't matter if it takes you a few flying hours longer than you thought it would, or more time than the next student who started the same day as you.

In fact, there are a number of reasons for the variation in time taken to first solo. The first is learning ability, of course. People vary in the rate at which they learn new skills, and some students pick up flying more quickly than others. Sometimes people struggle with one aspect of the course; I have known of students who simply couldn't manage take-offs, or who constantly made too high an approach to landing during the transition. But so what? None of this really has anything to do with how good they will be in the longer term, and sometimes older and/or slower people learn more slowly but have the common sense and maturity to be better pilots than their faster, younger colleagues. As a slow learner myself, I sympathize with anyone who's champing at the bit to go solo and who finds they seem to be taking longer than anyone else, but it really isn't important.

A second factor involves practical considerations. Medicals have already been mentioned, and students who are held up in that area often have to continue with later exercises, going solo when they legally can. Then there is the weather, particularly in Great Britain. Especially if you are ready for first solo during the winter months, there may simply not be a suitable day weather-wise. Sometimes students wait for weeks, if not months, and again it may be possible to go on with more advanced exercises in such a situation.

Finally, the type of helicopter may make a difference. It is not always the case, but students learning on the twitchy little R22 may take longer to go solo than those learning on something more stable and forgiving, such as the Enstrom 280 or the Schweizer 300. But it is often said that if you can fly an R22 you can fly anything, so again, don't worry about it.

Instructors need to be careful that everything is just right before they send students solo, because flying the helicopter alone will be very, very different from doing so with the instructor sitting in the left-hand seat. With no-one there, the weight and centre of gravity of the helicopter will alter quite a bit. During take-off, the cyclic will need to be further forward and well over to the left to compensate for the lack of weight in the left-hand seat. You will need to be really proficient in your take-off technique, and raise the collective very carefully, bearing in mind that due to the reduced weight the helicopter will also become light on the skids and lift off the ground very much sooner than you expect.

Some flying schools put a weight under or in front of the left front seat, to compensate a little for the different feel and make it easier for the student. This is perhaps a good idea, but at some point you will need to learn to fly with varying weights on the front seats, and maybe now is as good a time as any. Also, some flying schools have a 'first hover solo' before the official Exercise 12 first solo flight, perhaps quite some time before it. This gives the student the opportunity to do some take-offs and landings alone before having to go off and fly a circuit as well. This may or may not happen at the school at which you are learning.

Most commonly, the first solo flight consists of one circuit of the airfield, although it could involve more than this. You will find that the helicopter climbs faster than when you had the instructor on board. Also, a lower power setting will be required for the cruise and descent, and the descent will be slower. But other than that, simply fly as you have been doing, and it is unlikely that you will have any problems. You will probably thoroughly enjoy it, and marvel at the fact that there is no-one sitting in the left-hand seat, and that you can finally fly a helicopter alone!

Indeed, for most people, first solo is the highlight of their flying career, and one that they remember for ever. I don't wish in any way to change that. But it should perhaps be emphasized that we are all different. For me, maybe because I already flew fixed-wing aircraft, my attitude was that it was no big deal, and I just wanted to get on with the rest of the flying course. And some people may have completely different memories, particularly if something goes wrong, which is unlikely but possible. So enjoy it, perhaps take the rest of the day off and celebrate, but don't worry if your feelings aren't typical or what you expected them to be. For you now have the rest of the PPL(H) course to enjoy!

First solo completed – and now the rest of the course to enjoy.

4 ADVANCED EXERCISES

EXERCISES 13–21

From now on lessons on more advanced flying with your instructor will be interspersed with solo consolidation flying. The exact order in which the later lessons and this solo work are done will depend on many things. Weather plays an important part, as it does in the whole of the PPL(H) course. Other factors, such as helicopter availability and how much time you have available, may also come into play; for instance, some of the navigation exercises may take a couple of hours or longer. However, we will look at the more advanced exercises in the order in which they are given in the syllabus.

EXERCISE 13: SIDEWAYS AND BACKWARDS FLIGHT

Both sideways and backwards flight are done at approximately hover height, and you may well have done a little of each informally as an extension of your hovering practice. They are not merely co-ordination exercises given to students, as some people seem to think, but are skills that are sometimes required when manoeuvring a helicopter, for instance when trying to park close to other aircraft. They are not all that difficult, and you will probably enjoy this lesson.

Sideways Flight
Initially you will probably do this exercise facing into wind, but as you become better at it the manoeuvres will be practised in other directions too. After a good lookout, you will simply hover-taxi the helicopter sideways. As you might expect, the cyclic will control your speed, the collective holds your height, and the pedals keep you straight. You move sideways at a walking pace, and you need to develop a scan, so that you are looking in the direction of travel, then forwards, alternately. And that's really all there is to it.

There are, however, a few things that many students find difficult in the beginning, as with all new helicopter exercises. Some people find it hard to keep moving in a straight line, and the easiest way to manage this is to use a ground feature. Place the nose of the helicopter along the edge of the field, or a clearly mown section, or on some other obvious line feature, and then keep it there as you move sideways. It may still take you a little while to keep travelling in a straight line, but at least you will then have something specific to aim for.

Move sideways at a walking pace. (Neil Harrison)

Sideways flight out of wind is harder of course, since the helicopter will try to weathercock into wind. But by this time you will probably be proficient enough at hovering to cope – use your feet!

Backwards Flight
Backwards flight, or backwards hover-taxying, is done at double the normal hover height, so the first thing you need to do is climb to around 8–10ft; this is to protect the delicate tail rotor. You raise the collective to climb to this height, then make a 90-degree turn to take a good lookout behind you. Then you simply make a small movement with the cyclic to start the helicopter going backwards, keeping it straight with the pedals. Again, it isn't that difficult, though you will find that if you move too fast the nose tends to drop, so you will need to keep the movement slow and under control. And operating out of wind will again mean you have a lot of work on the pedals – get used to it; it's what helicopter pilots do!

Once you have mastered flying both sideways and backwards you should be able to use a combination of these techniques to fly the helicopter in any direction, in or out of wind. Your instructor may now give you some interesting challenges to improve your skill, such as hover-taxying around a square, always facing the same direction, so that you will move forwards, sideways, backwards, then forwards again. Always remember to keep a good lookout, and to climb a little before moving backwards. But overall, you should find this an enjoyable and not too taxing exercise.

EXERCISE 14: SPOT TURNS

Spot turns will probably not be completely new to you, since you will have had to turn the helicopter at least part way round in order to look behind you before flying circuits. However, completing turns in both directions, and doing so accurately over a fixed position on the ground, will probably be something you have not done before.

Spot turns will not be completely new. (Neil Harrison)

Left Turns

You will start off with turns to the left as these are much easier, unless you are flying a helicopter with clockwise-rotating rotors, in which case right turns will be done first. The lever controls your height, the cyclic controls the position on the ground and the pedals are for your rate of turn.

To do a left-hand turn you look to the right first to make sure that no-one is about to fly towards you from the direction you will be turning away from, then start the turn. For the first quarter of the turn you will need quite a lot of pedal input and the helicopter will try to weathercock into wind. After that you will need to ease off on the pedal as you continue the turn. You will have to co-ordinate the lever with the pedals of course, and move the cyclic into wind as you turn. So there is quite a lot to do, and good co-ordination is required, but you will have that by now.

Hopefully you will be learning these turns initially in light winds, as in stronger winds spot turns are really quite challenging. So if you do end up trying to do them for the first time in more than a light breeze – and sometimes we have to make do with the conditions as they are – don't be too hard on yourself if you find them difficult. Persevere, and practice makes perfect.

Right Turns

Right turns are a whole different ball game! They are much more difficult than left turns in anything other than a very light breeze, and you may well struggle with them. You also need to do them very slowly and carefully, and use left pedal to stop the helicopter turning too fast. You may also need to lower the lever to prevent the helicopter climbing.

Why are right turns so difficult? Part of the reason is that at a certain point in the turn, and with the wind from a particular direction, the tail rotor could cease to function properly. This may be due to vortex ring on the tail, which is when the wind acts sideways to prevent the tail rotor working. (Vortex ring will be explained in more detail under Exercise 15.) Tail rotor problems may also be due to the fact that the helicopter is turning too fast with high power being applied, and the tail rotor simply cannot cope. This is known as loss of tail rotor effectiveness (LTE), and is something you should always be wary of in conditions where a great deal of power is needed – but don't worry about it too much for now. Whatever the precise cause, you can feel as though you have run out of left pedal, and you could be unable to stop the turn. This is clearly not recommended! So right-hand turns should always be done slowly and with care, and if possible, particularly when you are flying alone, it is safer to always turn to the left.

Turns Around the Tail Rotor

As part of this exercise you may well do turns around the tail rotor. What you do is place the helicopter's tail in the centre of a circle (it helps if you actually have a definite point where you can place it), then move in a 360-degree turn around it. This is basically a combination of sideways hovering and spot turns, and it is an excellent co-ordination exercise. It is really quite difficult, so don't worry if you can't do these for quite a while. You will find it easier if you go slowly and break the exercise down into its component parts – move sideways a little, then turn, then repeat both movements. When you are downwind the helicopter will tend to drift, and you may well lose your position completely and have to start all over again. As I said before, practice makes perfect, and when you can do them, these are great fun.

Why do we do these turns around the tail anyway? Well, to a certain extent it is just a good co-ordination exercise, but the technique is also used if you are landing in a small confined area, and want to check the terrain around you for obstacles. You place your delicate tail rotor in the middle of the area, then move around it. I had never done turns around the tail in earnest until I did some flying in Russia many years ago with a very gung-ho military instructor. He made me land vertically in a tiny clearing surrounded by 200ft trees, and the first thing we did after landing was hover around the tail to make sure we knew exactly what was around us that we might need to deal with when departing. So it does have a definite use.

Your instructor may also give you other co-ordination exercises, both to improve your skill and give you confidence, and also to show you what helicopters can do. I sometimes used to get my students flying figures of eight. These are good practice, but should be done quite slowly and carefully.

You may at this point be getting fairly confident – which is good – but you need to bear in mind that all sorts of difficulties can arise if you start trying to do manoeuvres like these too quickly without more experience. You could find yourself reaching translational lift speed unexpectedly, when your helicopter will suddenly climb without you expecting it. And another phenomenon you could encounter, which we've mentioned now and then, is vortex ring state. This will be discussed in the next section.

EXERCISE 15: VORTEX RING RECOVERY

As a helicopter pilot, I have spent a significant amount of time explaining to people that helicopters do not just drop like a stone if the engine fails. I tell the nervous and cynical – who are sometimes my trial lesson students – about autorotation. I explain how the pilot lowers the collective to initiate a descent so that the up-flowing air keeps the rotors turning, and tell them that this allows the helicopter to descend faster than normal but under control, and to land safely. I state quite categorically that helicopters just do not fall out of the sky under any circumstances whatsoever.

However, this is not quite true. There is one aerodynamic state that can cause an uncontrolled and irrecoverable descent – or to put it more bluntly, a crash. This is vortex ring. Sometimes considered as the equivalent of a fixed-wing aircraft stalling, vortex ring state is a condition of powered flight in which the helicopter descends into its own downwash. This means that the air around the rotor blades will be turbulent and moving in all directions: since it is this airflow that normally produces lift when it is flowing smoothly, the result is that the helicopter will be literally unable to fly. Under such conditions the helicopter will descend at an extremely high rate, eventually 2,500ft/min or more. It will randomly yaw, pitch and roll; there will be buffeting and juddering of the airframe, with eventually total loss of control and possible structural damage – if the aircraft hasn't hit the ground first. I have seen a video of a helicopter crashing due to fully developed vortex ring, and the aircraft did indeed appear to just fall out of the sky. It was extremely sobering, to say the least.

Obviously, this is a state to be avoided at all costs. For this reason vortex ring recovery is a separate exercise in the PPL(H) course. Entry and recovery are demonstrated and practised extensively at a safe height. The idea is that you learn how to recognize it, and also to recover from it should it ever occur accidentally.

Three conditions all need to be present for vortex ring to occur:

- There must be an induced flow through the rotor disc, which means that you must have power applied.
- There must be a flow of air from below, so the helicopter must be descending.
- You must have very low airspeed.

To give you an idea of the numbers involved, you should assume that it is dangerous to simultaneously have power applied, be in a descent at over 300ft/min and have an airspeed of less than 30kt. So just remember 'the threes'. This actually gives you a bit of a safety margin, but helicopter types vary, so don't rely too much on that margin. And remember, any two of those three are alright, so don't worry about low airspeed at altitude or steep descents; just make sure all three conditions are never present.

In practice, one situation in which you need to be careful of vortex ring is the approach to the hover, which is why when you were learning this you were taught to keep coming forward and down very gradually until your rate of descent was below 300ft/min, and to go around if for any reason you couldn't do that. If you were to do what many students try when first learning transitions – slow down and try to descend more steeply – all the three conditions above would be present. Another likely time for getting into vortex ring is when practising more advanced downwind manoeuvres, when you can tend to estimate your speed from the ground rather than the instruments. The third likely time is during recovery from autorotation, if you allow the airspeed to get too low. I never used to understand this, so in case you too have that problem, let me explain in more detail. During autorotation, there is no possibility of vortex ring as there is no power applied, even though you are in a descent. However, during the recovery you pull in the power, but are also still descending. So unless you have been careful to keep up your airspeed, all the conditions for vortex ring would be present.

You will do the vortex ring exercise with an instructor at a safe height, probably around 2,000–3,000ft. You will first come to a hover, then initiate

Be careful of vortex ring during the approach to the hover.

a descent. You will then pull in the power, and at a certain point the helicopter will start to shake, pitch and roll, and the rate of descent will increase.

To recover, you need simply to remove one of the three conditions mentioned above. The easiest way, and the one usually used, is to move the cyclic forward to increase the airspeed. Another method would be to remove the power – to put the helicopter into autorotation. But normally you simply increase speed, and the juddering stops.

You will probably try this exercise both facing into wind and downwind, and you will find that it's actually quite difficult to get into vortex ring when facing into wind. Downwind it can be frighteningly easy in certain wind conditions, which is one reason why you have to be so careful when doing downwind manoeuvres. However, the aim of this exercise is not to see how good you are at getting into vortex ring! It is to give you a good understanding of it, and to make sure you recognize the symptoms of incipient vortex ring and recover early, since fully developed vortex ring is very hard to get out of and can cause structural damage to the helicopter, even if you manage to recover before hitting the ground.

One of the problems with this exercise is that some students can find it hard to believe that anyone could actually get themselves into vortex ring without realizing it. After all, when doing the exercise you do sometimes find that it is quite difficult to persuade the helicopter to get into it. And of course you're careful when doing transitions to the hover and autorotations, aren't you? So it's easy to think that it just won't happen to you. Therefore it is important to understand the real-life situations that can actually lead to this happening.

In any type of flying, problems occur when we are not looking out for them, and this is most likely when we are overloaded or distracted. Passengers can inadvertently cause such a situation. After you have got your PPL(H), you may well encounter a situation when a friend wants to take photos. Knowing nothing about helicopters, he or she is likely to expect you to put the aircraft in the ideal position: 'Down a bit, now right, can you slow down a bit more, can you get a bit lower.' You'll want to help, so you'll slow down, trying to manoeuvre as requested. But your eyes are now out of the cockpit, you've lost track of the wind direction . . . and suddenly you're in incipient vortex ring. Getting out of it should be easy, of course. But perhaps you happen to be downwind, you were a little low to start with, and you recognize it a little late – the outcome is unlikely to be good! So bear this in mind now and don't let it happen to you.

I speak from experience here. Like most of us, there was a time when I thought accidental vortex ring was something that only happened to other people. But twice in my flying career I've been a little too close to it for comfort. The first time was as a fairly new PPL, when I was flying into a rally in a large

Passengers can cause you to get distracted. (Neil Harrison)

field. I was orbiting, looking for a good landing site, my passenger was waving at friends on the ground, everyone was watching the helicopter and enjoying themselves – and suddenly I found myself in a high hover, without realizing it. Now there's nothing wrong with being in a hover at altitude, so long as you are careful. But you do need to be aware of it, so that you don't suddenly find yourself downwind and starting to descend without realizing it, as that's when the trouble can start. In this case it didn't – but it could have done.

The second time was much more recently, when I was doing a flight test in a new helicopter type, which involved air-to-air photography. The photographer in the other helicopter knew exactly what he wanted us to do and I was struggling to comply, working hard and flying very slowly in an unfamiliar type. Suddenly the extremely experienced instructor accompanying me, who had barely touched the controls up to then, grabbed the cyclic and moved it forward. 'It's OK', he responded to my enquiring look, 'You were getting into vortex ring, that's all.' We were? I hadn't even realized! Well, I'd like to think that his greater experience just meant he recognized the signs slightly earlier than I would have done. But it was still food for thought, as they say.

Finally, there is another type of person who worries incessantly about things, and he or she may find this whole exercise unnerving. Some students are really scared of doing vortex ring recovery, or even discussing it. If this applies to you, try not to panic. You do need to know about vortex ring if you are going to fly a helicopter, but as long as you fly sensibly, you are very unlikely to get into it inadvertently.

EXERCISE 16: ENGINE-OFF LANDINGS

This exercise should not be too difficult, as you will already have done Exercise 7, 'Basic Autorotations'. At least, you should have done. Sometimes the two exercises are combined, so don't worry if that is the case at your flying school. But in Exercise 7, if you were doing it 'by the book', as it were, you will have simply learned to do the entry into autorotation. In this lesson you will learn how to control the helicopter during the descent, select a spot to land, and actually carry out an engine-off landing to the ground.

At least, that is what you are supposed to do. In practice, you may recover to a low hover. The reason for this is that things can easily go slightly wrong in the last couple of feet, particularly in the R22, on which most of us learn. They won't go very far awry, and as long as you flare at approximately the right height, all will be well, and you would definitely walk away from a real engine failure if you got this even approximately right. In fact, in the R22, the skids and seats are designed to collapse in a hard touchdown, acting rather like the crumple zones of a car in a road accident. This means that even if the helicopter were to be destroyed, the pilot and passenger would survive unscathed – as long as you land vertically. However, such an outcome is not a great idea during training! We do like to finish this exercise with a helicopter that can be used again, and it would certainly get rather expensive if a new aircraft were to be needed for every engine-off landing exercise! So in some flying schools the rule is that you recover to the hover, and some instructors prefer to do this.

Does it make any difference? This is an issue that is discussed *ad infinitum* by instructors and examiners, but you honestly don't need to let it concern you. From your point of view, it makes no difference, although personally I found that when I eventually did an 'auto' to the ground – I was originally taught by an instructor who recovered to the hover – it gave me much more confidence that it could be done. So try to make sure you get the experience of doing at least one engine-off landing to the ground during your training, even if it means flying with a different instructor in order to do so.

You are likely to do this exercise in the circuit, at normal circuit height. You will start off by doing exactly as you did in Exercise 7 – on the spoken command from your instructor, you lower the lever, hold the attitude and apply right pedal. You then close the throttle, although again, the instructor may take care of this. After all, the aim of this exercise is to make sure that you could survive a real engine failure, and in such a situation you wouldn't need to worry about things like closing the throttle. You then select a 65kt attitude (this may vary slightly with different helicopter types) and aim for a selected spot on the airfield. At around 40ft you begin a gentle and progressive flare – don't flare too hard! Look well ahead, then at 5–10ft you level the helicopter and raise the lever. You will then either recover to a hover or, if doing the 'auto' to the ground, you will come to a run-on landing, and will need to use the pedals to keep the aircraft straight.

You are likely to do the engine-off landing exercise in the circuit.

This is straightforward to talk about, but harder to do, at least in the beginning, as quite a lot of co-ordination is needed for the flare and landing. But there are certain things you can do to make everything a little easier. As I've often said earlier, one important point is to relax. Engine-off landings can seem very scary, but remember that you have an experienced instructor, who will have done loads of these, sitting next to you. Also, you do have an engine, and if anything seems to be going wrong it is extremely easy to open the throttle, go around and try it again. So the fear many people feel when doing engine-off landings is really unnecessary. I remember, as a very new instructor, doing this exercise with a somewhat nervous student. As we lowered the lever, the rotor RPM seemed to stay lower than I had expected, though still within the normal range. This turned out to be because we had very little fuel and, both being small women, we were very light. However, I didn't realize that at the time, and said to her that I'd rather recover, do something else, and find out afterwards what was going on. I simply did this from a safety point of view, but we were never in any real danger and I knew it. She, however, worried about it all for months afterwards, something that I found out eventually from another instructor. So remember, you have a helicopter with a usable engine; you're just practising!

The next important point is to look well ahead all the time. There is a tendency for students to fixate on the instruments, and also to look at the ground as they approach it. This looking at the ground causes what we call 'ground rush', or the ground appearing to rush up and meet you. Looking well ahead prevents this rather disconcerting feeling. Of course you do need to keep an eye on the instruments, and develop a scan in order to monitor your airspeed and RPM, but you can probably scan fairly naturally by now.

Knowing when to enter autorotation to reach your landing site is always difficult, so don't agonize too much if you struggle with this. It will depend to a large extent on the strength of the wind, and you will get better at it with practice in differing wind conditions. In fact, as with everything in helicopter flying, practice makes perfect when it comes to engine-off landings. Also, there are certain things you can do in order to cover more or less ground while descending, but you'll find that out in the next exercise, 'Advanced Autorotations'. For this lesson, you just want to learn to reach approximately the right place, flare and land – don't try to run before you can walk.

There are a few other points to be mentioned, for interest if nothing else. In a helicopter with a governor, it is usually left on. However, in the R22 at least, some instructors prefer to turn off the governor, switching it on again at the last moment. The only advantage I can see to doing this is that the throttle can be closed more easily with the governor off; if you have it on, then you do need to make sure that the engine RPM is below 80 per cent, or the throttle will open itself again. But leaving the governor on means that you have less to do in those vital last few seconds when flaring and landing. It's swings and roundabouts really, and your instructor will probably take care of this side of things anyway. Again, it's something for instructors and examiners to discuss when they're bored! But I remember wondering about all this as a student, so that's why I'm mentioning it.

Finally, it should be noted that real engine failure is an extremely unlikely occurrence. Those that do happen tend to have been caused either by running out of fuel, or by forgetting to use carb heat in a helicopter with a carburreted engine. Also, you would usually have some sort of warning if the engine was likely to fail, so that you could well be able to land normally; it is rare for an engine to just suddenly stop. So do bear in mind that this is just an exercise, and try to enjoy it. This is possible, even if it doesn't feel that way now. In fact, once you start to get the hang of them, practising engine-off landings is great fun. I remember a very high hours instructor saying to me when I was a student that he would happily do them all day, and after a few years as an instructor I began to feel that way myself. But it shouldn't have taken that long. Try to enjoy them now!

You might find yourself learning engine failure in the hover during this exercise, although you may already have done that when learning to hover. Different flying schools vary as to when and where this is fitted in, and it doesn't really matter. If you want to read about it, see the end of Exercise 8 for a few details.

EXERCISE 17: ADVANCED AUTOROTATIONS

You will now have practised autorotations fairly thoroughly, both to a 500ft recovery and to the ground, or at least to the hover. So you will have realized that it is actually quite difficult to estimate how much ground will be covered when descending, especially as you might start from different heights above the ground and be coming down in various wind conditions. Indeed, by this time you might well be thinking that if you had a real engine failure and put the helicopter into autorotation, it would be extremely hard to estimate where you would be likely to land.

It is quite true that picking a landing site and knowing that you can reach it before lowering the lever and entering autorotation is quite difficult. But don't worry; you're not going to attempt that yet, though you will be quite soon. And in fact you'll never be picking a site, lowering the lever and sitting there hoping you make it, just like that. You can vary your speed and rotor RPM, as well as make turns, while coming down, in order to reach the area you are aiming for. And the purpose of this particular exercise is to show how changes in airspeed and rotor RPM, as well as turning, can be used to alter the distance covered over the ground.

It could be hard to work out where to land. (Neil Harrison)

Basically, if you slow the helicopter down in autorotation you cover less ground, and if you speed it up then you travel further. Lowering the rotor RPM – though obviously not by much – will also enable the helicopter to cover more ground. And turns will enable you to reach an area closer to you than would otherwise be possible. All these techniques can be combined in whatever way is necessary to reach a landing site. That's really all there is to it. However, in this exercise you will probably fly at specific speeds and rotor RPM settings, so that you can learn how to do it and see just how much difference it makes. It will also give you some practice in manoeuvring the helicopter in autorotation, and hopefully a degree of confidence in what might sound like a horribly complicated thing to do.

Techniques vary, but in order to see how much ground is covered, you will most likely start each autorotation from directly above the same point on the ground, using an obvious feature like a hedge at the side of a field or a large tree, although anything that can be clearly seen and identified will be fine. You need to be facing into wind. You will then enter autorotation and recover at the same height above the ground for each autorotation type, noting how far you travel in every case.

Minimum Rate of Descent Autorotation

Instructors can differ as to the order in which they teach the different autorotation versions, but it is highly likely that the first one you will do will be the Minimum Rate of Descent Autorotation, as this is very similar to what you have already done in earlier exercises. At a specific height, after doing your HASEL safety checks (your instructor should have shown you these), you will lower the lever, hold the attitude and apply right pedal as usual; you will then adjust the throttle and select the attitude that gives you the helicopter's minimum rate of descent; in the R22 this is the 53kt attitude. You should note this rate of descent, which in the R22 will be around 1,650ft/min, and also note how much ground has been covered by the time you start the recovery. The recovery for all autorotation variations will be the same – at 500ft you select the 60kt attitude (or the appropriate one for your helicopter type), open the throttle, raise the lever and start the climb as usual. This should all be fairly straightforward.

Range Autorotation

The next type you do will probably be the Range Autorotation. Again, you lower the lever; then you push the cyclic forward to select the 75kt attitude. The rate of descent will speed up to around 1,800–2,000ft/min, but the angle of descent will also change so that you will cover more ground. Take note of how much difference it makes, since despite what seems to be accepted wisdom, in my experience, unless you start from very high up, you really don't travel all that much further. However, you do cover a little more ground, so it is a technique you could use if necessary. You recover in the usual manner, starting at 500ft.

Extended Range Autorotation

The next technique is the Extended Range Autorotation (called Max Range in some textbooks). Here you select the 75kt attitude as before, then raise the lever slightly to lower the rotor RPM, to 90 per cent in the R22 or R44, or to whatever your instructor tells you is appropriate if flying another helicopter type. Of course you need to do this with care, and ignore the rotor RPM horn blaring at you – some instructors pull the rotor RPM circuit breaker before doing this exercise, which is quite a good idea. You will cover even more ground than before, but again, I've found that it really doesn't make all that much difference. Recovery is done as before, but you must lower the lever to get the rotor RPM back to normal before doing anything else.

Constant Attitude Autorotation

Next comes the Constant Attitude Autorotation. You enter as usual, then flare quite aggressively to reach a 35kt attitude. This time you will find yourself coming down very steeply, with very little ground being covered. It's quite dramatic, and some students feel a little as though they're falling out of the sky. But try to relax, and you will get used to it. This autorotation is normally used at night or in poor visibility, so that it can be completed without a flare close to the ground in conditions where it would be hard to flare accurately. But it is a useful tool during the daytime too, to reduce the distance covered. This is my preferred way of varying the distance travelled when aiming for a specific landing site – there is more on this in the next exercise. However, if using this technique in earnest you should revert to a normal autorotation by around 500ft above the ground, so that you can flare and land in the usual manner. In this exercise, you will recover as normal at 500ft, selecting the 60kt attitude for the climb as usual.

Zero Airspeed Autorotation

A more dramatic version of this is the Zero Airspeed (or Low Airspeed) Autorotation. After entering autorotation you flare aggressively and select the minimum airspeed possible, below 20kt (zero airspeed is actually quite difficult to achieve). You will need to maintain the heading with the pedals, as you will be almost in a high hover, and you will have to control the rotor RPM carefully. The helicopter's rate of descent will be extremely high – probably 'off the clock', and you will be coming down vertically, and you might definitely feel as though you're falling out of the sky! In a strong wind the helicopter will actually travel backwards, so this is one way of reaching a landing site directly below you if there is enough wind. You will have to recover earlier than for the other autorotation types, as you need about 500ft to get back to the normal 60kt flying speed. Why do you have to get your speed back? Remember the conditions needed for vortex ring – you are now descending, you are about to apply power, so you need airspeed – or you might find yourself landing quicker and harder than you expected! This type of autorotation is not easy at first, though not as difficult as it sounds. To be honest you are unlikely to ever need to use it in earnest. However, it is useful to practise, and it might well be the only way you could land in some situations.

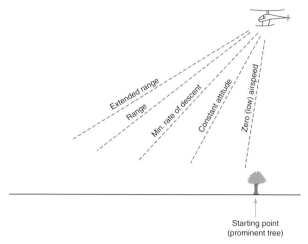

Distance covered during different autorotation types.

360-degree Autorotation

The final autorotation type you will do will be a 360-degree autorotation. In a light wind it would be impossible to reach a landing site directly beneath you using a Zero Speed Autorotation, and this would be a more appropriate technique. You enter autorotation, select 50–60kt, then roll on the turn. If flying from the right-hand seat, it is easier if you turn right, as you will have better visibility. The helicopter's nose will tend to drop after 180 degrees, and if doing it for real it is quite difficult to do the turn accurately without losing sight of where you intended to land. However, again it is a useful technique to learn. Recovery is done by rolling out of the turn and climbing as normal.

You may well do the Advanced Autorotations exercise over a couple of sessions, and to be honest you really can't have too much practice at this sort of thing. As well as enabling you to become more experienced at handling the helicopter in autorotation, it will give you a great deal of knowledge of how it works at different speeds and in various situations. However, some people find anything to do with autorotations difficult and a bit frightening, right up until the end of the PPL(H) course, and even afterwards. If this is you, don't beat yourself up over it. But do try to relax and enjoy these sessions, for they really can be a great deal of fun. Again, as I mentioned earlier, you do have a working engine, and can open the throttle if anything seems to be going wrong.

This exercise is designed to give you the skills and knowledge required for the next exercise – practice forced landings into a field of your choice.

EXERCISE 18: FORCED LANDINGS

You may be glad to hear that this is the last of the autorotation exercises in the syllabus. On the other hand, you might actually be starting to enjoy engine-off flying by now. But whatever your feelings about it, by the end of this session – or, more likely, two sessions – you should be able to make a safe autorotative landing into the field of your choice, both as an exercise and in an emergency.

This lesson actually puts together all of the previous autorotation exercises, so that you have all the skills to land successfully in the highly unlikely event of an engine failure. As I've said before, it should be emphasized that with modern engines, engine failure really is a rare event. Also, if an engine is going to fail, it is unlikely to do so suddenly; it is far more common for it to falter, lose power or give you some other sign or prior warning that something is amiss, thereby allowing you time to get on the ground in a reasonably relaxed manner. Sudden engine failures are almost always caused by fuel starvation, or 'carb' icing in piston engines, so if you pay attention to those two factors, you shouldn't ever have one.

Nevertheless, engine failure is always remotely possible, so you ought to be able to deal with it. One of the most important things to do is always bear in mind that possibility when you are airborne, and fly defensively. For instance, low flying may be fun, but it doesn't give you a lot of time to act if the engine should fail – far safer to be at 1,500ft above ground level, or more. Also, avoid flying over city centres or large areas of woodland; it doesn't take much longer to go around them, and it's much less dangerous should anything go wrong.

It is sensible to avoid flying over woodland or city centres, in case the engine fails. (Neil Harrison)

Moving on to the actual Forced Landings exercise, you should be aware that you will probably do this in two parts over two sessions, or even more. Probably – though not necessarily – you will spend the first sortie looking at all of the important points involved in making a successful forced landing. Then, during the second session, it will be a case of anything goes; your instructor will call 'practice engine failure, go,' or something similar, and you will need to make a successful forced landing – or prove that you could, since you'll probably recover and go around before reaching the ground.

A word about the second of these sorties first. Back in the dim and distant past when I was learning to fly, instructors tended to close the throttle suddenly to signal to the student that he or she needed to make a forced landing. The first the student knew about it was when the low rotor RPM warning horn went off. However, if the student didn't lower the lever quickly enough in these circumstances, they could both be in trouble, and I've heard that a few accidents were caused by using this technique. So 'throttle chops' are now generally frowned upon, at least when flying the R22, in which you don't have a great deal of time to get that lever down before the rotor RPM decays catastrophically. Your instructor may still practise them, especially if you fly another helicopter type, but it's fairly unlikely; a verbal warning tends to be used these days.

While we're on this topic, in the event of a real engine failure, how long do you actually have to get the lever down? Various times are bandied about, particularly in the case of the R22, where one hears figures quoted of one second or less. This causes people to think that either R22 pilots must have superfast reactions, or that the helicopter type can't be safe. However, flaring as you lower the lever raises the rotor RPM and gives you more time. If you lower the lever and flare simultaneously, you have around seven seconds in which to act. That may not sound like very long, but try counting slowly up to seven, and you'll realize that it should be enough. So you shouldn't need to worry about this aspect of things as much as the scaremongers would like you to.

Back, then, to the exercise. In the first session you will learn the sequence of events: enter autorotation, turn into wind, look for a field, and use one or a combination of the techniques you have learned in order to get into it. You make a 'Mayday' call if you have time, but it's fine to abbreviate it. By 300ft above the ground you should have the helicopter level and be looking to land safely. You turn off various switches like the fuel and master switch, if you have time and can reach them.

Entering autorotation is absolutely the most important point, of course. If you don't do that, nothing else will be of any use. So you need to lower the lever quickly, but under control of course, and flare at the same time. Then hold your attitude, and decide where you need to go. Now: you always, always, always know the direction of the wind when you're flying, don't you? If you don't, then you should make sure that fact changes from now on. You can find out which way it is blowing from things like ripples on water or smoke, or the fact that birds always take off into wind – a useful bit of information that I only learned quite recently. But to be honest, you don't want to be messing around after an engine failure looking for smoke or birds! Take a note of the wind direction before you take off, and unless you're in the hills or have flown a great distance or are in the midst of drastically changing weather conditions, it's likely to be nearly the same.

Next, you need to look for a field – or failing that, any piece of flat ground. Now, you'll probably be taught about the '5 Ss': size, shape, surrounds, surface and slope. Yes, you would love a big field, with a long approach, no obstructions, a good surface and completely flat. But you won't have time to look around too much, so you may have to settle for less than perfection. A few absolute no-nos are wires on the approach or right across the field (unless you can land parallel to them), high crops and steep slopes. Wires are almost impossible to see from the air, but you can see the posts. As I was once told on a safety course 'A wooden sticky-uppy thing with no branches or leaves is certain to have wires attached to it.' High crops make judging the flare before landing almost impossible. And of course you can't land safely on steeply sloping ground. So some things need to be avoided, but remember that if you're starting from around 2,000ft, you're likely to only have about 45 seconds to descend, so you can't spend too much time looking for the perfect field.

Look for a field, or any piece of flat ground, for a forced landing.

How will you get into your chosen field? Well, you've learned a series of techniques, but there are a few basic points to bear in mind. Firstly, don't aim for a field that is too far away; it's much, much easier to lose height than to stretch the glide. To lose height you can make turns or reduce speed, and in my opinion slowing down works much better. In fact, you can alter the speed almost continually during your approach, so long as you get it back to about 65kt by 300ft above the ground. Another way of doing things, particularly in a rural area with a selection of good fields, is to keep travelling at 90 degrees to the wind, i.e. on a 'base leg', until you are at the right height and position, then turn into your chosen field. But you will lose height in the turn, so don't leave things too late if you use this technique.

If you enter autorotation downwind, you will need to make a 180-degree turn before doing anything else. And if the only place to land is directly beneath you, you will need to decide whether to use a zero speed autorotation, which will work in strong winds, or make a 360-degree turn, which will be necessary in light winds. But although it is good to practise these, they are difficult techniques, so don't use them for real unless you have absolutely no alternative. And as already stated, you shouldn't need to if you fly sensibly.

You should make an emergency call at some point, giving at least your call sign and position. Your instructor may well let you forget it during the exercise, at least in the early stages. You should also turn off the fuel before landing, but of course you won't do this when practising, and in any case it is difficult to reach the fuel shut-off in the R22 if you are flying from the right-hand seat. Again, if doing this for real you might turn off the mixture and the master switch, and tell your passenger(s) to adopt the brace position, but you won't be worrying about that for now.

This all sounds complicated, but in fact you have already learned the relevant techniques. It's really just a case of putting it all together in a practical situation. And when it comes to the second session – if your instructor teaches things in this way – you should actually find that you know what to do. However, you could encounter a psychological problem here. It doesn't happen to everyone, but a typical reaction to an emergency, even a simulated one, is for one's brain to appear to slow down or freeze, In other words, just when you need to be using 110 per cent of your skills and concentration, you can't seem to do very much. I have several times had minor emergencies in the air, and on each occasion, just when I needed to be really sharp, my brain felt like cotton wool.

The best way through this is to take a couple of deep breaths and just carry on. Accept it as natural and don't panic, as that merely compounds the problem. Bear in mind that one of the reasons that we practise emergency procedures so much is so that the right actions can become automatic, or nearly so, and eventually you will be able to do them even when not feeling your best. You will also learn to recognize your own personal reactions to an emergency, and this is a useful thing to know and understand. In any case, after enough practice engine failures, these disconcerting reactions may well stop, or at least become less intense, which is one of the reasons for doing this exercise in the first place. In fact, you may actually come to enjoy it!

Finally, don't assume that you have learned everything there is to know about forced landings after this exercise is complete. It is always worth reading more, talking to people, and going on any safety or emergency courses that are held in your area. Knowledge is power ... particularly when it comes to helicopter emergencies.

EXERCISE 19: STEEP TURNS

Up until now you will have been doing turns at about a 20-degree angle of bank. However, there may be times when you will need to turn more steeply than this, perhaps to avoid other aircraft. Steep turns are also a good handling exercise, and they teach you a lot about how helicopters work.

After doing the HASEL checks, you pick a suitable feature outside the cockpit in order to maintain your position and prevent disorientation. You then roll into a 30-degree angle of bank. As the angle of bank increases, you will find that you need to add more power in order to remain level and not descend. You must maintain the correct speed – around 70kt – with the cyclic, and also make sure you use the pedals to keep the helicopter in balance. When you roll out of the turn you lower the collective to decrease the power. And that's really about all there is to it.

Roll into a 30-degree angle of bank for a steep turn. (Neil Harrison)

However, most students encounter a few difficulties with steep turns, particularly at the start. The first one is that for these turns you really, really need to take account of the offset seating, and pick a reference point in front of your nose. You will have learned to do that before, when doing Exercise 6. But when doing ordinary turns you can get away with not worrying about this too much. Although your flying won't be all that accurate, it probably won't make a great deal of difference, and neither you nor your instructor may realize that you've forgotten all about the offset seating problem. But if you use something in the middle of the windscreen as a reference point during steep turns, there will be trouble. In fact, you are likely to end up heading for the ground at high speed when turning in one direction, and slowing down and climbing quite dramatically in the other! This is definitely not a good idea, so this exercise is a good way of making sure that your turning technique is correct.

A word about what can happen if you get things very wrong. If you do inadvertently allow the speed to increase a great deal before your instructor intervenes, you should reduce the angle of bank before raising the nose. This is to avoid the possibility of mast bumping – the condition that occurs when the helicopter's main rotor hub makes contact with and deforms the main rotor mast, which was discussed under Exercise 6. This phenomenon tends to happen in conditions of low 'g' such us pushovers (pushing the cyclic abruptly forward in order to descend), but any drastic misuse of the controls, particularly at high speed, should be avoided to prevent the possibility of your running into it. It can only happen when flying helicopters with teetering rotor heads such as the R22, R44 or Bell 206, but these are the types on which most of us learn.

Another phenomenon you want to avoid at all costs is retreating blade stall. This occurs when helicopters go too fast, and it is the main reason why no rotary machines can travel as quickly as fixed-wing aircraft. At high speeds the advancing blade's airspeed will be extremely high, while that of the retreating blade will be very low. Eventually the latter will have an airspeed that is too low for it to fly, and the blade will begin to stall. The symptoms of this are vibration, and a tendency to pitch nose-up and roll towards the retreating blade. You are very unlikely to experience this in a steep turn however much you misuse the controls, but it's not impossible, and should it start to happen, you need to recognize the signs and decrease speed before doing anything else.

Don't start getting worried, or scared to attempt steep turns, because of the above. Helicopters are very safe machines so long as they are flown correctly and you don't attempt anything too extreme. However, it is worth mentioning these possibilities, since some people finish the PPL(H) course without ever having heard of mast bumping or retreating blade stall, and you do need to know that they can occur.

Maximum Rate Turns

You will also do Maximum Rate Turns, which are flown at 60kt and 45 degrees of bank. The technique you will use is the same, but you must allow the speed to decrease to approximately 60kt before applying extra power. Again, you will need to fly correctly using the right visual cues, or you really could find yourself getting this completely wrong. But as with everything else, practice makes perfect. You are not likely to use max rate turns in earnest very often. The most likely time for them would be if you had inadvertently flown into cloud and needed to do a 180-degree turn to get out, or if you needed to take avoiding action to avoid hitting something. Hopefully, you won't ever be in either of these situations.

Can you do even steeper turns than this? It really depends on the helicopter type, as well as the pilot's skill of course. Some rotary aircraft are almost aerobatic and can do extremely steep turns, particularly those with rigid rotor head such as the Bölkow Bo 105. Apparently, in the R22, turns of up to 60 degrees of bank are possible, or so I have heard. I remember talking to a very experienced instructor who had tried them, and he said that after 60 degrees the helicopter started to descend no matter what he did. But 45 degrees is the most you will do for the PPL(H) course, and for most of us, this is quite enough!

Steep Autorotative Turns

The final part of this exercise is steep autorotative turns. Again, these are done at 60kt with a 45-degree angle of bank. You will find that the rotor RPM will increase in the turn, and you will need to control that with the collective. You also have to use the pedals to keep the turn balanced. The rate of descent will increase significantly, but other than that there is really nothing particularly unusual about this manoeuvre. Again, you are unlikely to need to do these very often. But if you were unfortunate enough to have an engine failure with the wind behind you, a steep auto-rotative turn would enable you to position the helicopter into wind as quickly as possible.

Some people find steep turns quite difficult and somewhat disorienting, especially in the beginning. If this is you, remember that as with all helicopter exercises they will become easier with practice – as I've said so often before. And if you find that despite all that you really don't like them, there is no need to worry too much. Not all pilots like aggressive manoeuvres, and that is fine. Although steep turns are something you need to know how to do, and learning them will definitely improve your helicopter handling, they are generally not used very much by the average pilot once the PPL(H) course is finished.

EXERCISE 20: PRECISION TRANSITIONS

Precision transitions are an advanced co-ordination exercise, designed to give you confidence when manoeuvring close to the ground. But they do have a definite practical application: in fact, I find that I use them quite a lot and so do many other pilots, depending upon the type of flying they do. Precision transitions are used as a means of getting around the airfield at a reasonable speed, while remaining close to the ground and under control. They mean that you don't have to hover-taxi slowly over long distances, and they are also an efficient way of crossing runways, if you need to do that at the airfield at which you fly. Finally, they are a good introduction to quickstops – these are the next exercise, and you may well do the two of them together in the same session, since many students learn to do precision transitions quite quickly.

After a good lookout, you perform a normal, gentle transition into forward flight. You then adjust the lever as usual, and push through flapback and translational lift. But instead of allowing the helicopter to climb as you normally would, you select a slightly nose-up attitude to keep the speed at around 40kt, and lower the lever to maintain the height at approximately 10ft; then you simply keep flying at this height and speed until you want to stop. To return to the hover, you gradually raise the nose to decelerate, at the same time lowering the lever, then raising it again as translational lift is lost. As the speed approaches zero, you gently bring the helicopter to a normal hover.

For a precision transition, keep flying at this height and speed until you want to stop.

Throughout the manoeuvre, the heading is maintained with the pedals, the speed with the cyclic and the height with the collective, just as you would in any other low-level or low-airspeed phase of flight. It is not a difficult exercise, although as with all new manoeuvres, some people find it hard in the beginning. But in fact you will find that you have done all the parts of it before, for the exercise simply involves a transition to forward flight, flying straight and level, then transitioning to the hover.

The only new thing that some students find a little disconcerting is the fact that all of this is being done very close to the ground and at speed. You may find that flying around at 40kt at low level feels very fast and possibly extremely scary. Some people, however, thoroughly enjoy it and become quite hooked on it, wanting to go everywhere in this manner rather than hover-taxiing. This is really not a good idea: although precision transitions definitely have their place, they should only be used when there is some distance to be covered and where there is no chance of hitting anything or needing to stop suddenly. This is because, as you will discover in the very next exercise, there is no way to stop a helicopter really quickly, and the name 'quickstop' is a misnomer.

EXERCISE 21: QUICKSTOPS

The quickstop is an advanced co-ordination exercise. It does have practical applications when practising low flying, perhaps for commercial pilots doing something like survey or agricultural work, or even for an ordinary PPL(H) being forced to fly low because of cloud. However, to be honest, I have rarely heard of it being used in earnest. But it can be; an acquaintance once wrote to me describing the landing after his commercial flight test. He described it like this: 'This was a little unconventional as ATC cleared us to land and asked us to expedite. A very fast approach was made followed by the mother of all quickstops, urged on by the examiner.' Needless to say, this is not always the way you end a flight test, and I suspect that it wasn't actually necessary, and that the examiner was really trying to find out about the chap's flying skills. But I suppose that something similar could happen at a busy airport, so you need to be prepared for it.

The quickstop: on a signal, you flare and lower the collective. (Neil Harrison)

The quickstop is usually started from a height of about 30ft and an airspeed of 50–60kt. On a signal from the instructor, you flare and lower the collective. Then, as the groundspeed approaches zero and you lose translational lift, you raise the collective, at the same time levelling the helicopter. You then select the hover attitude and power, and come gently forward and down to the hover.

That, at least, is the 'book' way of doing it. In practice, most students find that they are all over the place the first time they try this manoeuvre, and the initial problem is usually that as soon as you flare the helicopter starts to climb, and you end up in a hover at 100ft or so. So you will probably find, particularly in a helicopter with a low-inertia rotor system like the R22, that you actually need to lead with the collective. And a large collective movement is required, while the cyclic flare should be gentle and progressive. Of course you will also need to keep the helicopter straight with the pedals while making these fairly aggressive movements of the other controls. So, as you will already have realized, there is a lot to do in a very short space of time. But as I said at the beginning, this is an advanced co-ordination manoeuvre, though one that you should be able to handle by this stage of your training. And to be honest, quickstops aren't really that hard, though it does take practice to find out just how much you need to move each control in order to maintain your height and not end up way above the ground, unsure of how you got there. This occurs often with beginners, so if it happens to you, don't worry about it too much: practice makes perfect. Also, one of the most useful things to bear in mind is that the name 'quickstop' is something of a misnomer. Quickstops take up a lot of space, and you really don't stop that fast. Many students try to hurry everything, and then it all goes pear-shaped. So when your instructor says 'quickstop, quickstop, go,' or whatever phrase is used at your flying school, don't rush; try to do everything in a fairly gentle, controlled fashion. Trust me; this makes it a lot easier.

Most of the difficulties in this exercise relate purely to co-ordination. However, there are other factors to be aware of. First, you need to remember that, as you approach the hover, two of the three conditions necessary for vortex ring will be present: low forward airspeed and power applied. So you don't want to allow the helicopter to descend, or the third condition will be present and you could quite easily enter vortex ring. But why should you want the aircraft to descend at that point, you might ask. Well, I once had a student who, when he found that he had climbed to around 60ft during the flare, thought that sitting there and allowing the helicopter to drop to 30ft before applying collective was a good idea! Needless to say, I quickly explained to him that this was definitely not the way to do it. The correct method is to tighten the flare and apply enough collective to come to a high hover, even if you are too high. You then come gradually forward and down until you reach a normal hover height. Making sure there is a little forward movement as you descend is another way of avoiding vortex ring state.

You will start off by doing quickstops facing directly into wind. After you become more proficient – and you will – you will learn how to do 'downwind quickstops'. Again, the name is a little confusing, as in fact you always finish facing into wind. The reason for this is yet again that you need to be very careful of vortex ring state when operating at low level, and this is particularly the case when you have low airspeed and the wind behind you. So with downwind quickstops you accelerate downwind, then either turn at speed and start to flare when within 30 degrees of the wind, or flare gently to around 50kt before turning and tightening the flare. These are respectively called the 'turn and flare' and 'flare and turn' techniques. In fact, I never learned them during my PPL(H), as they take up a great deal of space and there simply wasn't room at the small airfield at which I did my course. I have heard of other students who have also missed them out. To be honest, they are rarely likely to be used in practice, and if you do need to take avoiding action when flying fast downwind, a steep turn is probably easier and safer. But downwind quickstops are in the syllabus, so you are very likely to be taught them.

Quickstops have another practical use. The flare at the end of a quickstop is very similar to the flare before landing during an autorotation. During the annual Licence Proficiency Check (LPC), which all private helicopter pilots have to do once a year, one examiner whom I know always goes over quickstops before doing autorotation practice, pointing out to the pilot the similarity between the two exercises. Many people find it easier to do this manoeuvre when practising a quickstop, partly for the purely psychological reason that it is not an emergency situation.

Once you have mastered quickstops you are likely to find that they are tremendous fun. I quite often demonstrate them on trial lessons, if I have a fairly adventurous student who isn't likely to be put off by seeing the helicopter being thrown around. They give you the feeling that you have mastered the helicopter completely, and that you can now do anything in it with impunity. And indeed, to some extent this is the case. However, perhaps this is the good place to mention the possible dangers of throwing helicopters around the sky without thinking about what you are doing. We all know about vortex ring state by now, and the dangers of cyclic pushovers, negative 'g' and mast bumping have been mentioned earlier. But one danger that is sometimes not pointed out at all to students is LTE, or Loss of Tail Rotor Effectiveness. This has been briefly touched on in the section of Spot Turns, but perhaps now is the time to look into it in more detail.

LTE is typically defined as 'a critical low-speed aerodynamic flight characteristic which can result in an uncommanded rapid yaw rate which does not subside of its own accord and, if not corrected, can result in the loss of aircraft control'. What that means in practice is that your pedals seem to stop working properly and the helicopter starts turning in circles. It has been incorrectly called 'Tail Rotor Stall', a phenomenon which according to experts doesn't actually exist! LTE occurs when the tail rotor is not able to produce enough thrust to stop the yawing of the helicopter. The tail rotor is not stalled; it is simply being asked to do too much, and it can't cope. Accidents caused by LTE typically occur at low altitude and low airspeed, usually when the pilot is distracted and doesn't make corrections early enough. Typically the problem occurs when a great deal of power is being applied to the main rotor and there is just not enough corresponding power available for the tail rotor.

Thus LTE is most common at stages of flight with high power require-ments, such as when flying at low airspeed and out of ground effect, or when the helicopter is being operated in a high hover. The situation could be exacerbated by high altitude or hot weather, since again, more power will be required. The other main factor affecting the situation is the wind direc-tion, as you will know by now that winds from different directions affect the tail rotor in various ways.

So how is LTE connected with quickstops? It isn't in any direct way, and the quickstop is a very safe manoeuvre. But if learning quickstops has given you a little too much confidence, perhaps leading you to think that you can do anything whatsoever in a helicopter, then you need to realize that you could run into this particular problem, especially when operating downwind in maybe a slightly unconventional manner.

When it comes to LTE, prevention is better than cure, so if you decide to sling your helicopter around at low level, try not to operate at low airspeed – particularly below translational lift speed – in stronger winds and/or with a tailwind. Also, avoid out-of-ground-effect hovering and situations demanding high power, such as low speed downwind turns. Always be aware of the wind direction and strength, and stay alert to changing condi-tions generally.

If you should ever be unlucky enough to encounter LTE the following recovery technique is recommended. Apply full left pedal, and simultane-ously, move the cyclic forward to increase the airspeed. This will move air past the vertical stabiliser, which will help to stop the rotation. If you have the altitude, lower the collective and reduce the power, since this will reduce the tail rotor thrust requirement. Then, as you start to recover, adjust the controls for normal flight – and start to breathe again!

Now, before you begin to worry and vow that you'll never get into a heli-copter again, remember that I'm merely pointing out the dangers of aggres-sive manoeuvres done incorrectly and without enough knowledge of how a helicopter works. You are unlikely to need this information just yet – and perhaps you never will. However, many people do little further training after getting the PPL(H), and never hear of LTE, so I did want to bring it in somewhere. But remember that if you know about the forces involved in LTE, you are halfway to preventing it. Staying out of low-airspeed high-power situations when possible, and concentrating 110 per cent if you decide to fly in these conditions, should mean that you never encounter this phenomenon. And if you recognize it, correcting action is quite possible and not all that difficult, at least in the very early stages. So enjoy your flying, now that you should be getting to a stage where you really can. But perhaps the end of this section is an appropriate time to mention that there are good reasons why most experienced helicopter pilots are very cautious and don't take unnecessary risks!

Take care if doing aggressive manoeuvres in helicopters. (Neil Harrison)

5 MORE ADVANCED EXERCISES

EXERCISES 22–27 AND THE SKILLS TEXT FOR THE PPL(H)

You are now entering the final straight, as it were! You basically know how to fly a helicopter, and you probably realize this yourself by now. You just have to learn about navigation, in other words how to go places without getting lost or inadvertently blundering into controlled airspace. This will be interspersed with more solo flying, plus a few more interesting advanced handling exercises. Then will come the final hurdle: the Skills Test.

EXERCISE 22: NAVIGATION

Early navigation exercises can come as a shock to many students. It feels as though there is so much to do, even more to remember . . . and the problem is that you have to keep flying the helicopter at the same time. Small wonder, then, that when they start navigation, many students start to feel that they have forgotten how to fly. They can work out where to go, or they can fly the helicopter accurately, but not both at the same time. Don't panic; as with just about everything else in helicopter flying, it gets easier with practice.

The main problem is that trying to find your way in a helicopter is very different from navigation in a light aeroplane. Fixed-wing aircraft are inherently stable; this means that the pilot can take his or her hands off the controls for a short period to look at the map, change radio frequencies or write something down. But in helicopters it is much more difficult to do this. You cannot let go of the cyclic in most small helicopters for any length of time, and in helicopters like the R22 you cannot let go of it at all, as you will know by now. So you have one hand – the left hand – with which you have to do everything apart from the actual flying. Many people find it almost impossible to write with their left hand, and folding maps one-handedly just can't be done. Also, helicopter flying requires constant attention; if you take your eyes and mind off things, you can suddenly find that you have climbed or descended several hundred feet – not a good idea if you happen to be in or near controlled airspace, for example.

Perhaps it is not surprising, therefore, that most students – and also some low hour pilots – think at some point that helicopter navigation is virtually impossible. I recently took a fairly advanced student on his first trip to a new airfield, and he appeared close to tears when we got back – the apparent juggling act of flying, map reading and talking on the radio had completely defeated him. I remember feeling that way myself, even after I got my PPL(H), and I asked a more experienced pilot how he did it. 'Fly low and look at the signposts', he told me … and I think he meant it! These days, many pilots invest in a GPS as soon as they get their PPL(H), and use it as almost their only means of navigation.

This is a pity, because although helicopter navigation is quite challenging, it is really not as difficult as many people think. In fact, in some important ways it is easier than finding your way in fixed-wing aircraft. First, helicopters can slow down, even come to a high hover if necessary, although the latter needs to be done very carefully so as to avoid the possibility of getting into vortex ring. So at times of high workload, such as when approaching an unfamiliar landing site, you can fly slowly and give yourself more time. I always tell students that when they're approaching the airfield they should slow down to around 60kt. This gives them more time to assess the situation and work out exactly how to approach and land. Helicopters don't stall like aeroplanes if you fly them slowly, so make the most of this fact.

Slow down when approaching the airfield.

Second, helicopters can land almost anywhere. This is worth remembering, even if it is not something that you do very often. It means that a diversion does not have to be to another airfield: if the weather is bad, or you really can't cope with the situation, find a suitable field, land, and then sort things out. The mere knowledge that this is possible can really reduce your stress levels, particularly in worsening weather or if things are going wrong. Once, as a solo student, my map unfolded completely and I ended up with a cockpit absolutely full of it. What was I to do? I suddenly realized that I could land and refold the map. In fact, I was close to my home air-field and knew the way back, so I didn't need to. But the point is that I could have done. Fixed-wing pilots sometimes have real problems because a door opens, or they realize that an item that they really must have is in the back of the aircraft and out of reach. In a helicopter, none of these are emergencies; you can sort everything out on the ground.

Next, helicopters have better visibility and are more manoeuvrable than fixed-wing aircraft. This means that if you are unsure of where you are, orbiting and trying to find something on the ground that you can then recognize on the map is significantly easier. Again, in such a situation you can fly slowly.

Most of the difficulties involved in helicopter navigation can in fact be solved by careful prior planning and cockpit management. If flying a helicopter, you need to plan as much as possible in advance, knowing that doing so in the air will be difficult. So your charts need to be folded in such a way that you can follow your whole route without refolding them. People sometimes wonder about the correct way to fold a chart. In my opinion there is no correct method, especially in a helicopter; you re-fold it appropriately for every flight. Some pilots also write down all the really important information, such as headings and times for each leg of their route, on the chart itself. This could mean that you don't have to bother with a kneeboard, and since writing things down in flight is fairly difficult anyway, this is a viable option. Personally I prefer using a kneeboard, as I don't like having too much written on my chart; it can get in the way of useful navigation information. The choice is yours, but if you use a kneeboard, be sure to get a narrow one specially designed for helicopters, so that it doesn't get in the way of the cyclic when you're flying. You also need to decide which chart to use. In general I prefer the 1:250,000 ('quarter mil') aeronautical chart, as there is much more detail on it, but if my planned route is so long that I have to keep readjusting the chart, then I use the 1:500,000 ('half mil'). Again, the choice is yours, but make sure you are really familiar with the symbols on both of the above, and also on 1:50,000 Ordnance Survey maps, which you will need if flying to off-airfield sites; you really don't want to be puzzling out the chart information while you're in the air. And bear in mind that you will need to be familiar with all these charts for the Skills Test.

'How do you write things down?' I can't remember how many students have asked me this, aghast at the mere idea of remembering all the information given to them by ATC. But it is really not that difficult to remember simple radio responses, as they normally only involve one or two sets of figures, such as QNH and squawk code, or QFE and runway in use when approaching an airfield. If there is more information than that, or if you really can't remember two sets of numbers, repeat back what you can, and then ask the radio operator to 'say again' anything else. If you plan to do that in advance, there is no need for stress and panic. It is also worth listening in on the frequency first, since quite often other pilots will be asking for

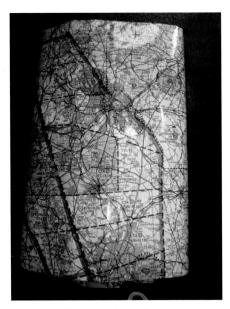

You can use either the 'half mil' or 'quarter mil' chart.

the same information. You can then obtain most of it at your leisure before you even press the transmit button!

There are two other alternatives: either learn to write with your left hand, or learn to use the cyclic with either hand. For a long time I did neither, and simply remembered any information I was given. However, a very high-hour helicopter pilot pointed out to me that complicated clearances had to be written down, and so eventually I would need to do so. I realized he was right, and worked towards finding a way. I can now use the cyclic with my left hand if I need to, which means that I can write things down if necessary. So it is worth learning to do this in the longer term, even if you can't do it immediately.

What about the basics – managing to fly while you look at the map and work out where you are, talk on the radio, alter frequencies and pressure settings, etc etc? Again, it helps to plan carefully and remember as much as possible in advance. Note any obvious features on your route such as large towns, isolated hills, or uniquely shaped water features or areas of woodland. Make a note of them on your kneeboard if necessary. If the visibility is good, you may be able to fly from one of these points to another. This could mean that you won't need to study the map to any great extent while you're in the air. I remember leaving a private site in Derbyshire one day to fly west, and the Wrekin – a large and prominent hill near Telford in Shropshire – was visible nearly 30 miles away. Since it was directly on my track, that was my navigation sorted for nearly the next half hour, and I could just enjoy the flying and the view. You can't always do this, but quite often it is possible. Or you can set your heading, then look for a prominent feature on your track and fly towards it; and when you get there, do the same thing again. This is far easier than constantly looking at the compass, and gives you more time to do anything else which needs to be done – and also to enjoy the flight.

Uniquely shaped water features are a good aid to navigation.

Much of navigation is similar whatever type of aircraft you fly, so don't forget to always know your wind direction, remember your regular aircraft checks, and plan carefully if you will be near controlled airspace. And if you are really unsure of your position for any length of time, call a large airport with radar, or Distress and Diversion on 121.5, in good time; they are there to help you, and being lost is not a hanging offence. But all of this is so much easier when you aren't struggling with the basics. Get them sorted out, and helicopter navigation can be relatively easy and lots of fun – and that's what it's all about.

For the remainder of this necessarily rather long section, I want to look at the important points involved in navigation for any flight, and what you will need to learn during the course. These can be divided into three parts: pre-flight planning, en-route navigation and arrival at the airfield.

Pre-Flight Planning

You can't do too much planning in advance. The more you can manage to sort out before you actually get airborne, the less there will be to do in the air, and the more time you will have for actually flying and even enjoying the flight. Navigation starts long before the flight, before you have even reached the airfield in some instances. You need to check the weather, read the NOTAMs and make sure that you have the relevant chart(s). Once that is all sorted, you can start to plan the route ... and don't skimp on this just because you may have seen more experienced pilots take off with nothing but a line drawn on the map, and sometimes not even that. When you have done your route plan, check it carefully; it is very easy to do something really stupid like reading the reciprocal (opposite) of your heading. So ensure that the whole thing makes sense.

Check the weather and read the NOTAMs.

If you are landing at another airfield, phone them in advance, even if PPR is not officially required. The airfield might be closed for some reason, or there could be problems that you don't know about. And while you're doing this, ask what I have found to be the most useful question for helicopter pilots going to new places: 'Are there any special procedures for helicopters?' It means that you'll know on arrival whether the airfield expects you to behave like an aeroplane and do an overhead join (more about that later) or if they're happy for you to make a direct approach, or something totally different. I remember the first time I went to Manchester Barton (now City Airport Manchester) and was told to 'follow the Manchester Ship Canal'. That would have been fine ... if I'd had any idea at all where it was. A prior phone call would have saved my confusion when approaching the airfield.

Make sure that you have the relevant radio frequencies, and book out with ATC, if that is something that needs to be done at your home airfield. Finally, if going any distance, and especially if landing away, take some supplies of food and water. This rarely gets mentioned to students, but it should. At some airfields it is impossible to get any kind of sustenance, and you can't fly well when you're hungry or dehydrated.

En-Route Navigation

When you start, this appears to be the really difficult bit. How do you look at a map all the time, know where you are, and still fly? The answer is that you don't. Set the heading from overhead the airfield (or another point if you have been recommended to do this), then note the time and your ETA at your first turning point. After that just check your route every few minutes or so, or when passing overhead some obvious ground features. Don't constantly look at the chart and try to work out what every single village or bit of woodland is. That way leads to mental overload and other problems. Try to fly accurately and at your planned airspeed, although if you're slightly off, it won't make much difference. If you follow the above rules, you should find yourself fairly close to where you want to be when it comes to making a heading change or other correction.

When approaching your turning point, if you find that you are off track, navigate to the correct point using one of the methods your instructor will show you. Turn on to the next heading, note the time and repeat the process.

This all works well unless you are genuinely uncertain of your position. If this happens, use the map to try to identify where you are, orbiting an obvious ground feature rather than simply blundering on, hoping you'll recognize something eventually. If you still can't work out your location, but you are close to a main road, railway line, or stretch of coastline, then fly along it until you can identify your position. If that doesn't work, set the radio to 121.5 and ask the Distress and Diversion cell to tell you where you are. As I said earlier, that's what they're there for! You can make it a 'Pan' (urgency) call, but it doesn't matter too much what you say, so don't worry about the correct terminology. Usually they identify your position so quickly that you wonder why you spent so long worrying about being lost. Remember, so long as you have a working radio set, you can always obtain assistance and you won't be lost for long.

If you are lost but near a 'line feature' such as a stretch of coastline, fly along it until you can identify your position.

Arrival at the Destination

During early navigation trips, your destination may be your point of departure – your home airfield. But later on you will be visiting other airfields, and you need to know what to do and how to land. If you have worked out as much as possible in advance, it should not be that complicated. However, going to a new airfield is always a high workload activity, so it is best to make your radio calls well in advance, and slow down to around 60kt to allow yourself plenty of time to work out the best approach and what else you may need to do.

This may end up being your first introduction to the strange (for helicopter pilots) procedure known as a Standard Overhead Join. This is the most usual way for a fixed-wing aircraft to join the circuit. You arrive overhead at 2,000ft, then descend on the 'dead' side of the airfield – the side not being used for circuits – crossing to the 'live' side at circuit height. It really isn't a helicopter procedure, but some airfields will expect you to use it, so you will need to know how to. As stated earlier, it is always a good idea to have phoned in advance, so that if you have to do an overhead join, you know about it and can go over precisely what to do. Otherwise, use whatever approach you are asked to, or choose your own. And remember to keep a very good lookout for other aircraft. Many fixed-wing pilots find small helicopters hard to see, so don't just expect them to avoid you.

It might sound strange, but make sure that you always positively identify the airfield at which you are planning to land. Believe it or not, it is fairly common for pilots to land at the wrong aerodrome, particularly if two airfields in close proximity have a similar runway layout. If something looks wrong from overhead, then it probably is, so sort things out before landing if at all possible.

Make sure you identify the airfield as your intended destination before you land there!

Other Points

Other things you will be taught are navigation in marginal visibility, and when and how to divert to another airfield or make a precautionary landing in a field. In addition you will learn how to use different scale charts, including 1:50,000 OS maps for finding off-airfield landing sites. And you will do a little radio navigation, using VORs and possibly other radio navigation equipment if it is fitted to your helicopter. Finally, you will do some solo navigation trips, which will probably be interspersed with cross-country flights with your instructor.

So there is much to learn. But don't despair. Although navigation is officially only one exercise, you will spend a number of hours working on it. Eventually you will come to enjoy it, for finding your way and going to new places is what helicopter flying is really all about. And although you may already have decided to invest in a GPS as soon as you have your PPL(H), remember that basic navigation is still a useful skill to have and one that many pilots find immensely enjoyable.

EXERCISE 23: ADVANCED TAKE-OFFS, LANDINGS AND TRANSITIONS

This exercise used to be called 'Operating out of Wind', for that is what you will actually be learning to do. Up until now you will have been taking off, transitioning, approaching and landing into wind, at least as far as possible. You should continue to do this whenever you can, both now and in your future career as a helicopter pilot. However, there are some occasions when manoeuvres have to be done crosswind or even downwind. Therefore learning when it is acceptable to do this, and how to achieve it safely, are included as a separate exercise in the PPL(H) syllabus.

Most students become familiar with hovering and hover-taxying crosswind and downwind fairly early on, since it is usually necessary to do this in order to get around the airfield. Hovering is slightly different depending on where the wind is coming from, and you may now learn how this works in more detail. However, the main points to remember are that the wind will try to push the aircraft downwind, and the tail will tend to weathercock into the wind. So you need to move the cyclic slightly in the direction of the wind, and you have to be very quick on the pedals, in order to keep the helicopter facing in the direction you want. This also applies when taking off and landing out of wind, which again is something that many students will have had to do.

This is not all that hard in fairly light winds, although it can become far more challenging if the wind speed picks up. In such circumstances it can often be avoided by hover-taxying sideways facing into wind, for instance, a useful trick that you should bear in mind if you haven't learned it already. However, downwind transitions, from the hover to forward flight and from forward flight to the hover, are much more difficult. This is why

You need to be quick on the pedals when hovering downwind. (Neil Harrison)

they are taught quite late on in the PPL(H) course, since very precise control of the helicopter is required. They are also only practised in light winds, usually of less than 10kt, although some people do suggest a higher limit of 15kt.

For the transition from the hover to forward flight, you raise the helicopter into the hover as usual. You then ease the cyclic forward very, very slowly. The main problem at this point is that the wind will blow you forward, but your airspeed will actually decrease for a while, until the groundspeed is the same as the wind speed. This may be easier to understand if some numbers are used. Suppose the wind is blowing at a speed of 10kt. As you lift into the hover, you have a rearwards airspeed of 10kt. However, as the helicopter moves forward, this airspeed decreases, so that when your groundspeed forward is 10kt, your airspeed is actually zero. Only then will the forward airspeed start to increase, but it will take you far, far longer than usual to acquire translational lift and enough airspeed to be able to climb away safely.

You might find this quite hard to follow in theory. But in practice it just means that you need a great deal of power, and that the power requirements of the helicopter increase initially since your airspeed is decreasing – remember that more power is needed to hover with zero airspeed. In addition your transition to forward flight will cover a great deal of space, since it is taking you so long to reach safe flying speed. So you don't do it unless you have a long runway or the equivalent amount of room. I still remember the first time I tried this as a student: I was amazed at just how much I needed to raise the collective to keep from hitting the ground. I could also hardly believe how great a distance we covered over the ground. But gradually you will pick up speed, and when you reach translational lift speed the power requirements will lessen, so that you can then start to climb away as normal.

You will probably fly a 500ft circuit, although this varies at different airfields. It is important to keep well out of the way of other circuit traffic, as you will be going in the opposite direction to them. But however the circuit is achieved, you will eventually be in a position to start the downwind approach to the hover. For this you again need a considerable amount of space. The approach will necessarily be shallow, and since you will again have the wind behind you and pushing you along, you will need to keep your airspeed quite low, usually around 30–40kt. Again, you are likely to be very surprised the first time at how much ground you cover, even with a light wind. You will need to keep a constant eye on the airspeed indicator, since it is essential to monitor your airspeed rather than your groundspeed in order to avoid getting into vortex ring. Particularly as you descend close to the ground, if you look at the terrain you will think you are going quite fast, when actually your airspeed may be becoming dangerously low if you still have a high rate of descent. But eventually, if you do everything carefully in the same way as for a normal approach, you will be able to come to a hover as usual, and land. Some people say that you should turn into wind at the end of a downwind transition, and I have seen this done by a very experienced pilot who was making a downwind transition into a confined area. However, this is quite a difficult manoeuvre and is only necessary if you are short of space. I never learned to do it that way, and I strongly suggest that you simply conduct out-of-wind operations in the way your instructor recommends, at least for the foreseeable future.

Your first thought when reading all of this, and definitely when practising it, might be 'Why on earth would anyone want to do downwind transitions at all?' It is an extremely good question, and in general, out-of-wind operations are to be avoided. However, sometimes they are necessary in real life. In some confined areas there may be high obstacles such as power lines or tall buildings, which mean that there is effectively only one way into or out of the site. In other instances there may be restrictions on where you can fly, particularly if you are going to a large fly-in or similar event. I remember flying in to Helidays, the annual helicopter fly-in at Weston-Super-Mare, and realizing that the instructions I had received from the organizers, which were to approach the landing site from the south or south-west so as to avoid over-flying certain parts of the town, meant that with the westerly wind that day we were highly likely to be approaching crosswind or downwind. It was not a major problem and all the arriving helicopters did it successfully, but it still would not have been my first choice of landing direction.

Of course, sometimes when landing at a private site you end up doing a crosswind or downwind transition unintentionally, since you do not always have any definite indication of the wind direction, and winds can be variable or changeable. I once flew to a friend's house for a visit. As a helicopter pilot and owner he had a windsock on his land, and he was directing me in on his handheld radio. It was a big field with few obstacles, and I had been

Sometimes there may be obstacles like tall buildings. (Neil Harrison)

approaching into wind, or so I thought. But as I approached the landing site my friend called to me, sounding slightly concerned, 'Be very careful; you've got a bit of a tailwind.' The wind had completely changed direction, quite suddenly. It was only about 7kt, so was not a major problem, but it was still a good idea for me to know about it before I landed.

These types of situations have to be considered on an individual basis. In another instance, when trying to use a long, narrow off-airfield landing site, I found that it was easier to land across the strip but into wind, rather than down its full length but with quite a strong crosswind. And in yet another case I refused to take some passengers to a rather challenging landing site with only one practical approach and departure direction, as I would have had a very strong tailwind on that particular day, and I considered the site to be outside of my capabilities in those conditions. Safety always has to come first.

In practice, you are not likely to use out-of-wind transitions very often, unless you fly to a large number of off-airfield sites. This is probably just as well, since in addition to requiring loads of power and space, they are also less safe in the event of an emergency. No-one wants to have an engine failure after take-off in any situation and they are, thankfully, extremely rare. But if I were to have one, I would far, far rather be facing into wind, than to have to either turn into wind at low level, or attempt a downwind autorotation. And I think that many of us would be fairly unlikely to manage either successfully!

When it comes to the approach to the hover, the same applies with respect to possible engine failures. But now you have the added difficulty of controlling the helicopter in anything more than a light breeze as your speed decreases. You will need to watch the airspeed indicator like a hawk in order to avoid vortex ring, at the same time trying to keep the helicopter straight with the pedals when it wants to weathercock into wind. You will also need quite a lot of aft cyclic to slow the helicopter down, which could mean you run the risk of striking your tail on the ground. Does this really sound like your landing of choice?

All of this means that you should be very aware of the wind direction at all times, and if possible make your take-offs, landings and transitions into wind. It is not essential, but it is certainly safer, and it will make your flying life a good deal easier.

But of course, there will be times when you will not want to do this for quite sensible reasons. Some years ago I flew myself to a fly-in at another airfield. It was a very successful event, with a large number of people flying in, practically all of them apart from me in fixed-wing aircraft. After having lunch and socializing, we all left at around the same time, which meant that the queue for departure on the one into-wind runway stretched halfway around the airfield. However, realizing that the wind was fairly light and that I had plenty of space, and of course not needing a runway, I asked for permission to depart crosswind in the direction in which I wanted to go. I can still remember the envious comments I received afterwards, as everyone saw me effectively jump the massive queue and set off homewards.

But then, this versatility is one of the reasons why we fly these wonderful little rotary machines, isn't it? So out-of wind-operations can definitely be one of your arsenal of manoeuvres, to be used safely and when useful or necessary; that is why they are taught. But do remember that they should be used with care.

EXERCISE 24: SLOPING GROUND

Among the general public, helicopters have a reputation as all-terrain vehicles that can take off and land just about anywhere; even some rotary pilots think that way. But although helicopters can indeed cope with a wide variety of conditions, they are really not all that good on slopes. Even slightly sloping ground requires care if a helicopter is to be operated safely, and landing on anything greater than a 5–7-degree incline is probably not a good idea unless it is absolutely necessary. This does not sound like very much, but if you have ever tried putting a helicopter down on a slope of that magnitude – and you may not have done so as yet – you will probably have found it so uncomfortable that you won't want to even consider attempting anything steeper.

So what are the problems associated with sloping ground? Firstly, there is the very real possibility that the rotors – either main or tail – might touch the ground. This is why you never, ever land facing downhill, since the delicate tail rotor could so easily come into contact with the slope. Facing uphill is permissible, but you do have to bear in mind that you run the risk of the main rotor striking something. Some rotor systems are nearer the ground than others to start with, but even in the case of the ones that look safe, rotor blades flap as they slow down. Therefore pilots usually land their helicopters across the slope, at right angles to it. But a special technique of landing and taking off is needed if we are to do this safely, and this is what you will learn in this exercise. This is primarily because it is very easy to turn a helicopter over when taking off or landing on a slope due to 'dynamic rollover', as discussed in the section on Exercise 9. But it is most important to realize that, while dynamic rollover is possible during any take-off or landing if the controls are mishandled, it is far more likely to occur when operating on a slope.

So why is this the case? Even if you are sitting on a very gentle slope, total rotor thrust will already be at an angle to the perpendicular. Therefore a rolling horizontal component will be present before you even start to move the controls. The pilot also has to lift off one skid at a time in order for the helicopter to take off vertically – there is just no other way to do it. Thus a pivot point is necessarily created about the skid on the ground, and with power applied: all the conditions for dynamic rollover will be present, unless the pilot is extremely careful. He or she may well not notice the danger since the helicopter still seems to be within normal limits of operation – and dynamic rollover can happen very suddenly. If it does occur, it is likely to be about the skid that remains on the ground – the uphill skid! Again, this is not what the pilot is likely to be expecting.

For this reason, sloping ground take-offs and landings are one of the most difficult exercises in the PPL(H) syllabus – or at least I certainly found this to be the case, and so have several of my students. This is why they are one of the last exercises in the course, and are not taught until you are fairly experienced at handling the helicopter. However, as I've so often said before, don't panic! The first thing to realize is that you have probably already done some sloping ground landings. At some point during the course so far you are likely to have landed and taken off on ground which is uneven, or landed in an area that you don't know for certain is absolutely flat. Your instructor will probably have told you to be extra careful, and to do everything very gently. Well, that could well have been your first operation on sloping or uneven ground. But you didn't know it, so you probably weren't worried about it. It is the perception of a slope that some students can find unnerving, so it is important to realize that this is merely a psychological effect.

To make things easier, you will practise sloping ground take-offs and landings on very shallow slopes at first. If learning on a helicopter that hovers left skid low, like the R22 and most other small training helicopters, you will probably land first with the left skid downhill, as this will be the easier direction. However, the order in which you do the exercise may also depend on factors such as terrain available and wind direction.

Landings usually come first, since dynamic rollover is less likely to occur when there is not much power applied. As for any landing, you establish a steady hover, then start to lower the collective until the uphill skid just touches the ground. At this point you stop! Then, as you lower the collective further, you need to move the cyclic gradually towards the uphill side, so as to keep the rotor disc horizontal. If you don't do this, the helicopter will start to drift down the slope. You continue doing this, co-ordinating the two controls carefully. Once both skids are safely on the ground you can lower the lever, but still taking care, as you need to check that the ground is solid and will not give way. I knew a pilot who landed apparently safely in the hills in mid-Wales, but as he was lowering the collective, part of the surface gave way and the helicopter overturned! Don't let anything like this happen to you. Finally, once on the ground, you can centralize the cyclic – and start to breathe again.

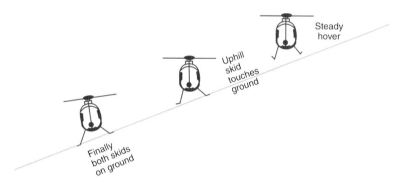

Landing on sloping ground.

For take-offs, you need to position the cyclic first, at the same point as it was when you landed … if you can remember that. You then raise the collective very slowly, so that the lower skid lifts off the ground, but in an absolutely controlled fashion. At the same time, you need to look well ahead, and gradually move the cyclic towards the centre so as to keep the rotor disc exactly horizontal. If the collective is raised too quickly, dynamic rollover could easily occur, and as already stated it will be around the uphill skid, since this is where the pivot point will be. If this looks likely, the collective must be immediately lowered, but not too fast or the helicopter could bounce and roll around the other skid. You must on no account try to lift off quickly, to get the helicopter away from the ground – this is likely to aggravate the situation. Once both skids are off the ground, you can centralize the controls and fly as normal, or try the whole thing all over again.

You may well think that this exercise sounds horrible! Without doubt, it is not easy in the beginning, and it is a definite test of co-ordination and concentration for the new helicopter pilot. It can also be a trial of nerves for his or her instructor, so if your instructor seems a little tense, please make allowances for him or her! But as with all helicopter exercises, practice makes perfect, and it will get easier as time goes on.

You will practise this exercise in all directions: right skid uphill, left skid uphill, and both skids uphill. As already stated, you never land with the tail uphill for safety reasons. You may also do landings at 45 degrees to the slope, which is something that can be useful on a very steep slope. You will then practise on steeper slopes to improve your skill and hopefully increase your confidence. But small helicopters cannot land on anything very steep. For the R22, while no official limits are quoted, around 7 degrees is probably the sensible limit.

Trying to land on too steep a slope can cause all sorts of problems, as I discovered once. I was instructing at an airfield that had an interesting area of sloping ground, where the angle of slope gradually got steeper as you moved downhill. I had a rather enthusiastic student at that point, who learned quite fast, and he had mastered the sloping ground operations exercise in quite a short time. Since we had a few minutes of the lesson left, I suggested that he try landing on a slightly steeper slope, then an even more challenging one. However, the particular portion of the slope that we were using cannot have been more than about 4–5 degrees when I realized that we had better stop, since when we landed with the skids facing uphill, albeit on wet grass, the helicopter made a definite attempt to slide down the hill. Needless to say, I took control and lifted us off immediately. My student definitely learned something useful that day – and so did I!

When are you likely to use these techniques in practice? Once you have gained your PPL(H), you probably won't deliberately land on sloping ground if you can avoid doing so. But operating on very slight slopes is something that every helicopter pilot needs to know how to do if he or she takes a helicopter to almost any off-airfield site. Such places are rarely completely flat, so unless landing on a prepared surface such as at an airfield, you need to consider any landing as a sloping ground one until clearly proved otherwise. Long grass can hide wheel ruts or small holes, and rain or mud can mean a normally level surface is no longer as it used to be. Therefore, you need to be ready to react appropriately if the situation is not as you thought it would be, and this is what you are really learning how to do in this exercise. If the slope is only 1–2 degrees, then while cautious handling of the controls is required, no particular change in technique is needed. Also, since helicopters generally hover with one skid lower than the other, if you land with the lower skid downhill you may not even notice that the ground is not level.

It should now be clear why we should always try to land somewhere reasonably flat if at all possible. This is not all that difficult during the sort of trips that most private pilots tend to do. Even landing at a private site or in a confined area, there is often a small part that is level, and it is quite easy for a helicopter to make an approach to a field or paddock, then hover-taxi around it in order to look for a relatively flat area. Therefore the ordinary PPL(H) tends not to use sloping ground techniques all that frequently, but it is something that you always need to remember how to do.

Of course, things are different for commercial operators such as police, search and rescue and emergency medical services pilots, who might have to land in some pretty extreme situations. So the next time you see one of them landing in some rough country, in the hills or somewhere else where the ground is definitely not level, you will realize that what they are doing is not easy and requires great care, even for very experienced helicopter pilots. It is even harder in helicopters with wheels, which stand more chance of rolling down a slope, unless you are flying a type in which the wheels can be locked. Luckily, these guys are experts. But for the rest of us, let's land on flat ground whenever possible, since we want to enjoy our flying and keep it safe.

Things are different for commercial operators, such as air ambulance pilots.

EXERCISE 25: LIMITED POWER OPERATIONS

The Limited Power Operations exercise (i.e. limited engine power output) is perhaps one of the most misunderstood lessons in the PPL(H) syllabus. It is not that the techniques involved are complicated, although of course some students do struggle with them initially. It is that many pilots fail to appreciate the real reasons for doing the exercise at all, even after getting their licences. They do not understand when they might use these techniques, when they should not be used, or the practical issues involved in putting them into practice in the real world outside the flying school.

The main aim of this exercise is what its name suggests: to learn what to do when the helicopter's available power is limited to such an extent that some normal operations are not possible. As a helicopter pilot, you may find yourself operating an aircraft in parts of the world where the engine power available is restricted for some reason. The most likely reasons for this to occur are because you are at high altitude, on account of hot weather, or both of these – the so-called 'hot and high' scenario. This is because hot weather and high altitude, or a combination of them, mean that air pressure is reduced, which reduces the power developed when the fuel/air mix is combusted in the engine. In the UK we have a temperate climate and no really high mountains, so British pilots are only likely to actually need these techniques if they have an engine problem. It should be emphasized that limited power techniques should never be used in order to operate the aircraft above its AUW (all-up weight).

The usual way to do this exercise is to have a simulated limited power situation by restricting the amount of manifold pressure available. The instructor will tell you that you can only raise the collective a certain amount, usually until the helicopter is just light on its skids. You will then push the cyclic gently forward so that the helicopter runs along the ground, gradually picking up speed until translational lift speed is attained. At this point the helicopter will be able to fly, so you can gently transition away into a climb. This is known as a 'running take-off'. You may also be taught a 'cushion creep', which you can use when there is just enough power available to hold a hover. This is very much like a normal take-off, but you need to stay close to the ground and do everything very slowly until you reach translational lift speed.

A similar procedure is followed when landing. Again, you will only be allowed to apply a fixed amount of power. You then descend, keeping just above translational lift speed until the helicopter's skids touch the ground. You then perform a 'running landing' by allowing the helicopter to run along the ground on its skids until it gradually comes to a halt. There is also the 'zero-speed landing', where the same technique is used, but you slow down further until you reach the ground cushion, then gradually lower the helicopter onto the ground. This technique is quite difficult to do in practice, and tends to only be used when the surface is not smooth enough for a running landing.

As already stated, some students find running take-offs and landings quite hard initially, since they seem so different from conventional helicopter manoeuvres. Ex-fixed-wing pilots, on the other hand, tend to have little trouble with them, as they are fairly similar to aeroplane take-offs and landings. But as with everything you have learned up to now during the course, they just take practice.

Towering and vertical take-offs, and vertical landings, are sometimes included in this exercise, and by rights they should be, since these involve limited power situations that you could well encounter for real in any

You keep just above translational lift speed until the skids touch the ground.

country. In order to do these, you will learn how to carry out pre-landing and pre-take-off power checks in order to ascertain how much power is available. You will then be able to use a set of pre-determined figures, which depend on the type of helicopter you are flying, to work out the capabilities of your aircraft and what type of take-off or landing can be used. These are an important part of learning about helicopters and power requirements. However, all of this may be learned during the Confined Area Operations exercise instead, simply because there is so much involved in the practical side of limited power techniques, but do bear in mind that power checks are not necessarily something you only use when operating in confined areas – they are definitely a part of the whole topic of power requirements.

This is something I learned for myself in the USA some years ago. Like most British helicopter pilots, up until then limited power operations were all a bit theoretical – something you learned but never really used. Then I left England and went off to the USA to do some 'hour building'. I spent three weeks based at Long Beach Airport, near Los Angeles in southern California, doing loads of flying and having a wonderful time. Then one day I decided to fly to the mountain airfield of Big Bear.

Big Bear is a ski resort, and was reputed to be a beautiful place. It had an airfield at an altitude of around 7,000ft. It was April, so the weather was not that hot, and the day in question was a typical pleasantly warm spring day. I was aware that no-one flew to Big Bear in the summer in a low-powered R22 helicopter, for you would definitely encounter the 'hot and high' conditions I had heard about, though never experienced at that time. But this early in the year it should be OK, shouldn't it? Actually, if I was honest, I wasn't quite certain. Luckily I realized how inexperienced I was when it came to mountain flying, and decided to take an instructor with me – always a good idea if you're not certain about the conditions or your own capabilities. In this case it turned out to have been a very sensible move.

Tim, the experienced instructor whom I asked to accompany me, was actually a little wary of flying to Big Bear, even that early in the year. However, he thought it would be alright, especially considering that we were both fairly small and light. Nevertheless, after checking the weather, we both sensibly went over the performance graphs for the R22 we were planning to fly. On paper everything seemed fine, with enough power margin for possible changes in the weather, so off we went.

It was a spectacular flight over 10,000ft mountains, with stupendous scenery. Everything went well, and as we flew over the hilltops, there was Big Bear airfield on the nose, exactly where it ought to be. I joined the circuit, turned on to final, and came to a hover, with no problems at all. But as I turned the helicopter out of wind in order to hover-taxi to our parking spot, the low rotor RPM warning horn suddenly came on. Looking worried, Tim immediately took control. Hovering extremely low to the ground in order to make maximum use of the ground cushion, he managed to manoeuvre the R22 just clear of the runway. But the collective was fully raised and the RPM warning horn was blaring continuously. It was clear that our little helicopter just could not fly in those conditions. I had never seen anything like it before.

It was a spectacular flight over 10,000ft mountains.

So what had happened? Well, clearly conditions had changed since we had done our calculations. Being later in the day, perhaps the weather had got warmer than we had expected or than the forecast had predicted. Either way, at 7,000ft we were 'hot and high', the air was thinner and without a headwind we could not hover. We shut down, with Tim looking extremely anxious and muttering about how difficult it would be for us to get away if things didn't change.

In my innocence I didn't quite understand why we had a problem. 'We can do a running take-off, can't we?' I asked him brightly. After all, I had learned to do all this stuff in theory, and actually I was quite looking forward to putting it into practice. So Tim explained to me the things that I hadn't learned during the Limited Power Operations exercise. Yes, theoretically we could do a running take-off. However, first we had to get the helicopter to the runway. Well … we could probably borrow some wheels, couldn't we? Yes, but then we'd have to park the helicopter at the end of the runway, ready to start up, and block the use of a popular airfield for the length of time it took us to start the engine, do our checks and be ready to depart. It was certainly possible, but hardly recommended. And next, Big Bear had a hard runway, with a reasonably smooth surface, but definitely not ideal for a running take-off. It certainly wasn't like the beautifully mown English grass where I'd practised my Limited Power Operations exercise a few years earlier. I began to understand why Tim looked so concerned. Clearly this whole limited power thing wasn't the piece of cake I had thought it was.

Luckily, by the time we had finished our lunch the temperature had dropped somewhat. We were able to hover, and Tim managed to lift the helicopter and hover-taxi carefully until we were facing into wind. Once we had a headwind things were better, and we were then able to make our way to the runway and transition away, using a gentle but normal take-off technique, close to the cushion creep technique that I had learned. Then we could finally breathe more easily and relax as we enjoyed another spectacular flight back to the lower altitudes of Long Beach.

I learned a lot about helicopter performance and the reasons for doing the limited power exercise that day. Learning about something in theory is very different from seeing it for yourself in practice, and it came as a great shock to me when I saw for myself that our helicopter genuinely could not fly. I also understood the limitations of the limited power techniques. I had assumed that if you had restricted power, you could always do a running take-off or landing – that was why you learned it, wasn't it? However, in practice you need to be positioned correctly, and have a lot of space and a good level surface in order to perform these techniques. If you don't have those, things will be a lot harder. You might have to start getting rid of passengers or fuel, or wait for better conditions. It is far, far better not to get into such a situation in the first place.

Therefore the most important aspect of this exercise is not necessarily to be good at the techniques, but to learn that helicopter performance and power are things you should always be aware of. Many pilots who live in temperate areas at low altitudes only do power checks if they are flying into confined areas when carrying passengers, if they do them at all! Despite the fact that at present all of this is something you will rarely need, you should remember that knowledge and understanding of power margins is a vital part of helicopter flying, for all of us.

EXERCISE 26: CONFINED AREA OPERATIONS

Helicopters can land almost anywhere! At least, that is the commonly held belief. Most people who are not familiar with rotary flying think that you can simply lift your helicopter into the hover, take off vertically and fly. Then, when you arrive at your destination, you come straight down and plonk the machine on to any old bit of ground.

Many new helicopter students start off thinking this way, but of course they soon find out that it just isn't true – and I'm sure you know this by now. In reality, confined area operations are quite difficult and can be dangerous, for there are a great many things that can go wrong. For this reason the confined area exercise is one of the very last lessons in the PPL(H) syllabus, and is not even attempted until the student is reasonably competent at helicopter handling.

Even after getting your licence, landing in a small space is something every pilot needs to attempt very cautiously. At the school where I trained for my PPL(H) and from which I used to hire helicopters afterwards, low-hours pilots were not allowed to do any type of off-airfield landing unless an instructor had seen the site and okayed it in advance. This was to prevent enthusiastic and over-confident new pilots from coming unstuck when trying to land in a confined area – as can easily happen.

So what is a confined area and what are the potential problems? Most importantly, how do you land in one safely? I've never seen an exact definition, but basically it is any space in which the flight of the helicopter is limited by obstacles. These obstacles may be terrain, such as a landing site among hills; they might be trees or bushes, or they could be houses or other buildings. They are highly likely to include electrical pylons and wires. These are almost impossible to see from the air, and flying into wires is a major cause of helicopter accidents. A confined area may be quite large, but be difficult to land in because of its shape, or the position of the obstacles, or the wind direction, or all of the above. Every single confined area is different and must be assessed and approached in a different manner.

So what are the possible difficulties? The first one, of course, is that you might fly into something or try to land on an unsuitable surface. This may sound unlikely, but obstacles are very difficult to see from the air. Steeply sloping ground can look flat, and fields sown with crops can look like meadows. As mentioned previously, wires represent a major hazard: I was taught that the first thing you must do before a confined area approach is ascertain exactly where the wires are – since there are sure to be some, somewhere! It was good advice.

The next potential problem is that of frequently needing to take off and land vertically, or nearly so. Yes, helicopters can do this, but it isn't particularly easy, and it isn't recommended unless absolutely necessary. In the admittedly unlikely event of an engine failure, it would be very difficult to land safely. Also, such landings require great care, as there is a very real risk of getting into vortex ring state. If this were to happen in a confined area with little room to manoeuvre, a crash would be almost inevitable. Next, you need to be very careful about power requirements, particularly in the Robinson R22 or similar small piston-engined helicopters that many low-hours pilots fly. You may have enough power available to land vertically in the area – but will you be able to get out again, particularly if the weather becomes warmer?

Let us now take a look at what you will learn during the actual confined areas lesson. It is important to note that this exercise is closely allied to the Limited Power one, and if you haven't learned about the power available for different types of take-offs and landings then, you will certainly do so now. It is most important to check this before each and every confined area landing or take-off.

Confined Area Landings

The first thing you will do before landing in a confined area is a reconnaissance, or 'recce'. This means you fly around the site, checking that it is suitable for landing. You consider what are often called the '5 Ss': size, shape, surface, slope and surrounds. You need to add another S in rural areas, for 'sheep', and yet another one in winter, for 'sun', as a low sun on the approach could really cause you problems.

The next thing you do is plan a low circuit, sometimes called a low recce, and fly it. This should include a dummy approach and a go-around, so that a close look at the actual landing site is obtained. Some people say to fly this circuit at 500ft above the highest obstacles; others recommend lower than this. It is best to do as your instructor tells you at this stage. Recommended speeds vary too, but generally it is best to fly the circuit at 60kt, slowing to around 40kt on base leg. The aim of this dummy approach is to find out if there are any problems you hadn't been able to ascertain from the air, such as hidden wires, holes in the ground, wind shear and so on.

Then, and only then, will you fly a circuit and land in the clearing. There are three main approach variations you can use. The first is a constant-angle approach, where you follow the same approach angle all the way to the ground. A double-angle approach is used when a constant angle approach would be unacceptably steep. In this case, a shallow approach is flown, then a steeper approach to the aiming point is used – carefully! The final type of approach is a vertical approach, which is used in small restricted areas, and of course must be done with extreme care.

In all cases, the approach is made to a high hover. You then do clearing turns about the tail – *see* Exercise 14 for more details – before landing. Landing is done cautiously, using the sloping ground technique if there is any doubt at all about the state of the surface.

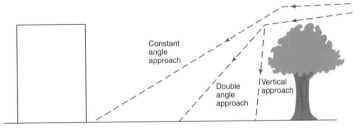

The different techniques for landing in a confined area.

Confined Area Take-Offs

Before attempting to leave the clearing, you need to check the power available, since you will need to do either a towering or vertical take-off. If there is any doubt at all, it is permissible to do a trial vertical climb to see if you have the power to avoid obstacles.

You then need to decide on a safe way to leave the area. It is good to take off into wind if possible, but if this involves climbing over obstacles or wires, it may be safer to leave crosswind or even downwind. Next you come to a low hover and climb vertically until you can clear any trees or buildings ahead. For a towering take-off you climb above them when you can do so at the best angle of climb speed, while for a vertical take-off you ascend vertically until above all obstacles, then move the cyclic forward to leave the area. The latter of course uses a great deal more power.

Does this all sound difficult? I hope so, because in a tight confined area, it is. Because of this, many private pilots rarely do confined area manoeuvres after getting the PPL(H). Indeed, if you hire helicopters from flying schools or clubs, some of these don't even allow it, so people fly to other airfields, or perhaps land on large, flat areas that aren't really much of a challenge. This is a totally sensible thing to do; 'make haste slowly' is always a good maxim in aviation. But it doesn't give new pilots much opportunity to extend their flying and learn how to do more. Also, I suspect that many of us hanker after trying some 'real' helicopter flying, involving manoeuvres like getting into really tight spaces. After all, that was why we wanted to fly helicopters in the first place, wasn't it? If we'd wanted to fly between airports, we could have gone fixed-wing and saved a lot of money.

I certainly felt that way, and fairly soon after getting my PPL(H) I was lucky enough to be able to have a go at this type of more challenging flying. As I mentioned briefly in the section on Exercise 14, I had the chance to try some helicopter flying in Russia with ex-military pilot instructors. And on the last day of my ten-day trip, I learned how to land in a really tight confined area.

My instructor that day was Sasha, an ex-war hero who had been shot down in Afghanistan and also once ditched over the Black Sea, or so I heard. He directed me to a tiny little clearing in the middle of a huge forest, telling me to land our Mil Mi-2 there. It looked difficult, if not impossible. The only

Many of us hanker after some 'real' helicopter flying.

way in was to fly overhead, then let down absolutely vertically from around 600ft. I had never done anything like that before, but I tried. However, I couldn't see where to land, as the large Mi-2 instrument panel got in the way. Sasha showed me how to come down vertically, keeping my aiming point diagonally off to the side, looking out to my left so that I could see where I was planning to land. It was difficult, and there seemed to be no room at all for error; in fact, there appeared to be hardly room for the helicopter at all. I struggled with it for what seemed like ages. Finally, trembling slightly from the intense concentration, I managed to come to a hover over what now turned out to be sloping ground. But my tired feet forgot about the required bootfuls of right pedal. The Mi-2, like most Russian helicopters, has clockwise-rotating rotors, which means right pedal is used when increasing power. I had become accustomed to the change over the preceding few days, but apparently not all that accustomed.

'Right pedal, right pedal, RIGHT PEDAL,' yelled Sasha, as I struggled to straighten the helicopter. Then, obviously thinking that I needed a clearer demonstration of what 'right pedal' meant, he took control, put in full right pedal, and took us in a spiral vertical climb up to 600ft, where he immediately handed over to me to try again. I was stunned. I would have sworn there wasn't room to turn the helicopter round in that space – but we still had a tail rotor, so there must have been. I was also really, really tired, and now I had to do it all again. I thought of saying that I'd had enough and that it was too much for me, but I just couldn't bring myself to refuse to do the sort of helicopter flying I'd secretly always wanted to try.

Sasha, meanwhile, looked totally unconcerned. He was chain smoking, hands and feet nowhere near the controls, as I wobbled dangerously near the trees on my second attempt. He opened the door to flick out the ash, and the door whipped out of his hand in the strong wind. He grabbed at it half-heartedly and missed, so he left it swinging in the wind. I wondered if this was the reason for my difficulty in descending vertically and hovering accurately. But it could have just been intense fatigue by now, for this gung-ho stuff felt like it was really a bit beyond my limits at that time. Anyway, I thought, at least there was a gap ahead of the clearing when we came to leave – and then I saw the power lines! There was no way in or out of this area except vertically.

Finally I managed to land on the designated spot. Sasha grabbed my cyclic hand and then roared with laughter; I was pouring with sweat. 'Helen, relax,' he said good-humouredly. And after making me manage the vertical take-off to clear the power lines, he directed me to a field for some of the very precise hovering practice that I so obviously needed. By the end of the hour – and it felt like much longer – I was exhausted, but elated. Overall, it was one of the best helicopter training sessions I can ever remember.

That hour with Sasha also taught my something far more important: that this sort of helicopter flying is best done with an instructor, or left to the experts. I had certainly enjoyed it, but it was definitely at the limit of my capabilities at the time, and it was not something that it would have been safe for me to do alone.

So if you want to land in a confined area after you get your PPL(H), do so, but take care. If at all possible, have a look at the site from the ground first. If it looks too challenging for you, never be afraid to refuse to land there. I have several times told people that the site where they wanted me to take them simply wasn't suitable. They've sometimes been annoyed, but passengers don't know about helicopter flying and therefore don't appreciate the dangers. It is always your decision, so don't be afraid of making an unpopular one.

One the other hand, if you manage to get the opportunity to extend your abilities by doing the type of flying that I did in Russia, do take advantage of it. I promise you that you won't regret it, and it will make you a better and safer pilot.

EXERCISE 27: INSTRUMENT FLYING

The PPL(H) syllabus includes five hours of instrument flying: learning to fly accurately by sole reference to instruments. Although it is officially the last exercise, you may well do it over several separate sessions throughout the course, perhaps when the weather is too bad for any other flying. So by the time you come to read this, you might have a pretty good idea of what instrument flying involves in practice.

Perhaps the crucial thing to remember about the instrument training exercise is that no-one actually wants you to put it into practice after getting your PPL(H). This might sound a little strange, but it must be emphasized that this exercise is not an instrument-training course. The purpose of it is just to enable you to do a 180-degree turn if you should happen to inadvertently enter cloud or an area of poor visibility, no more.

The purpose of Exercise 27 is solely to enable you to get out of cloud.

Instrument flying is very difficult, particularly in small, unstable helicopters such as the R22. The reason is that our perception of our position in space depends on the senses, and a large proportion of it is visual. This means that if you can't see, you don't know whether you're flying level or not. It is very, very easy to misinterpret the attitude of the helicopter, and you can feel as though you are in a steep turn when in fact you are flying straight and level – a condition so common that pilots have given it a name: 'the leans'. Other strange sensations can occur too; strobe lights can cause vertigo, and flying in and out of cloud can cause particularly confusing feelings and perceptions.

For these reasons, it is important to completely trust your instruments and ignore your senses when doing instrument flying. They represent the outside world, but on a smaller scale. So movements of the controls must be small and gentle, and you need to learn to interpret what the instruments are saying about the outside world, and be able to make correct adjustments. This can be very hard to do when all your senses are telling you the complete opposite of what the instruments are indicating, which can easily happen.

Having said all of this, some students find the instrument flying exercise surprisingly easy! People vary, but a proportion of students, particularly those who perhaps tended to keep their attention inside the cockpit too much when flying visually, don't find it that difficult to concentrate on the instrument panel during this exercise. This means that although the only requirements for the Skills Test are that you are able to do a 180-degree turn on instruments, the five hours of the syllabus set aside for instrument training are often used to acquire a lot more skills – climbing and descending, turning and maybe even practice forced landings and recovery from unusual attitudes. This is not a bad idea, for if you were to fly inadvertently into cloud in real life, recovery from unusual attitudes is very likely to be what is actually required! But anyway, many students thoroughly enjoy this exercise, don't find it all that difficult, and come away thinking that all this fuss about instrument flying is actually a load of baloney!

The thing to understand is that instrument flying as it is done during the course is very different from flying in real cloud. Many schools teach the instrument part of the course with the student just wearing foggles, which are special goggles designed to cut out peripheral vision and only allow you to see what is directly in front of you – the instrument panel. In a fixed-wing aircraft, foggles do indeed cut out most of a pilot's vision. But in a helicopter, with its all-round view, they don't – you still have quite a lot of visual cues. For this reason, some schools attempt to put up screens on the helicopter as well. But doing this in such a way that the student cannot see outside but the instructor still can is very difficult. Either way, you do end up with some visual cues, even when you think you're concentrating 100 per cent on the instruments. Thus students can find themselves believing that instrument flying really isn't all that difficult. They think that if they happened to fly into a cloud, there would be no real problem.

When wearing foggles, you can only see the instrument panel.

I found out the difference between simulated IMC and the real thing during instrument training for my CPL(H), which is of course more extended than that for the private pilot's licence. I was wearing foggles, and we had actually erected screens as well. I was quite certain that I could not see anything outside, and I was focusing completely on the instrument panel – or so I truly believed. After a short period I began to get the sort of spatial disorientation discussed above that is so common in instrument flying; I felt as if I was in a steady right-hand turn, although my instruments told me that I was flying straight and level. It was annoying, but basically not a problem, and I just carried on flying.

Then suddenly my perception of turning increased dramatically. I felt as though I was in a very steep turn, going almost round in circles. I began to get dizzy and nauseous, and I found it hard to concentrate. I told my instructor, and I said that if it continued I thought I'd have to stop. But then, just as suddenly, the feelings of turning lessened, and I assured him I was alright. My instructor was more put out than I had expected. 'Helen,' he asked me sharply, 'Are you quite sure you can't see anything outside?'

I assured him that I was absolutely certain. I had only been able to see the instruments for the whole of the session … or so I thought. He then told me that the short period during which I had felt so ill had been the exact time during which we had flown through a small cloud. I had had no idea of this, but it seemed that my body and senses had somehow perceived the difference between simulated and real IMC.

Pilots who have never flown in real cloud are often unaware of the dramatic difference between this and instrument training. Flying in cloud can be totally, completely disorienting. Many people have an idea in the back of their minds that they can fly by the seat of their pants, at least to some extent, but in IMC you can't, not at all. Spatial disorientation can give rise to 'the leans', as it did for me, to the extent that you can feel as though you are hanging out of your seat in a steep turn, or turning in circles, when you are actually flying straight and level. You have to rely totally on your instruments, although your senses are screaming at you that they are wrong. It's horrible! And in addition, when doing it for real, you will need to know where you are, navigate, maybe talk on the radio. Even if only trying to do a 180-degree turn and get out of cloud, you need to monitor the compass or direction indicator to know when you've actually made that turn. It's not easy, and anyone who says it is either hasn't tried it or is lying. And even if you're trained to do it, instrument flying requires constant practice, and degrades faster than almost any other skill.

Why, then, is this exercise in the PPL(H) syllabus at all? Over the years there has been a great deal of discussion about this, and in fact many instructors feel that it shouldn't be there. But others feel that pilots who inadvertently fly into cloud must be given a chance; they should have all the techniques possible at their disposal. Also, the skills learned during this exercise help with general aircraft handling, particularly when flying with little or no horizon, for example in the mountains, at night, or when crossing water. I remember, fairly soon after getting my PPL(H), crossing the Channel to France in conditions of marginal visibility, where the horizon just about disappeared for several miles. Although I wasn't flying by sole reference to instruments, I really needed to use them to quite a great extent, and having been trained to do so helped considerably.

What, then, does the PPL(H) instrument flying training include? You will be taught how to develop a scan, going from the attitude indicator (AI), which is your 'master instrument', to another dial and then back again. I was always taught that you should never look away from the AI for longer than two seconds, and you are only scanning the other instruments to check that they are backing up what the AI is telling you. You will learn that there is a lag between control input, variation in aircraft performance and changes on the dials, and this is one of the things that makes instrument flying so hard. You should acquire a basic knowledge of how all the instruments work. You will then try to do all the helicopter basic manoeuvres on instruments although, as stated above, all that is required for the Skills Test is the ability to do a turn to get out of cloud. You will of course do all of this over a series of sessions.

Finally, I will say again that you should bear in mind that learning to fly helicopters on instruments is a useful skill, just so long as you know what it should and should not be used for. Personally, I feel that all student pilots should be taken for a flight in real IMC, just once, to let them feel what it is really like. Ask your instructor if perhaps this is a possibility. It ought to convince you that instrument flying is not the piece of cake you perhaps thought it was, but should be left well alone for those who are qualified to do it.

THE SKILLS TEST FOR THE PPL(H)

You're almost there! You've now completed all the exercises for the helicopter private pilot's licence. You will spend a few more hours doing revision and general practice with your instructor, and then all that remains is to prove to an examiner that you can fly competently and safely.

This is easy to say, but at this point even the most calm and phlegmatic of students may have an attack of nerves. I always did; in fact I was dogged by flight-test nerves for the whole of my flying career. It may help you to realize that the idea of a flight test is indeed pretty scary for most of us, and to be a little worried at this point is actually normal. Indeed, many students feel that they can't possibly be good enough, so it is important to realize that the examiner is not expecting perfection.

So what does the test involve? The examiner will expect you to complete the 'A' check on the helicopter, using a checklist. He will want you to start it up as you normally do, again following the checklist. You should do all checks out loud if possible, so that he can actually see that a good standard of airmanship is being maintained throughout the test. He will then take you through all the manoeuvres you have learned throughout the flying course.

The most important thing to remember is that the examiner wants you to pass. He will do everything possible to ensure that you feel relaxed; you will not be intentionally pressured in any way. If anything goes wrong during the test, he will give you a chance to have another go. The aim is to make sure that you can fly safely, and small inaccuracies will not preclude success. And whatever you might read or hear about what you are supposed to do, or whatever limits the rules say you are supposed to fly within, there is always room for examiner's discretion. So never give up mentally just because you think that you aren't flying well enough. That is a decision for the examiner to make, not you.

There are various things you can do in advance to give yourself the best chance of passing. Try to make sure that you feel fully prepared, both physically and mentally. Ensure that you know the syllabus, that you've done your revision, that you've had a good night's sleep. It may also help to remind yourself that your instructor wouldn't have put you in for the test if you weren't ready, and that it is very rare for anyone to fail.

The trouble with all this is that it doesn't always help. Many people simply cannot fly at their best during test situations, no matter how much they are reassured. Indeed, some are so overcome by nerves that they can hardly perform at all. I was one of those, and if you are too, perhaps it will help a little if I tell you about a flight test I undertook, which appeared to go disastrously wrong. It was the final test for my Commercial Pilot's Licence or CPL(H), but what happened could just as well have occurred had I been taking the PPL(H) Skills Test.

As I said earlier, I get horrendously nervous doing exams, particularly practical ones. I've been this way all my life, but it actually seems to get worse as I get older. It's bugged me throughout my flying career, and I've never really done well on any kind of flying test. When it came to my CPL(H), this had actually compounded the problem, as it meant that I now actually expected to feel tense and to do badly. It was an on-going problem, and I'd tried everything to deal with it, but nothing helped very much.

I prepared well in advance, and convinced myself that I felt ready for the test. In fact, I almost convinced myself that I wasn't scared. But I was actually suppressing the fear, and that made it worse, as it often can. When it came to the helicopter start-up, this soon became obvious. I was using the checklist, and doing things that I'd done hundreds of times before. But somehow, I forgot to put in the clutch after I'd switched on the engine. It's about as basic a mistake as you can make on an R22, but I did it. So I sat there, and the examiner sat there, until eventually I realized what I'd done – or rather, not done. At that point, I came clean and admitted to the examiner (and myself) that I was extremely nervous. I then took a couple of deep breaths and carried on. But I was by now in such a wound-up state that I could hardly fly. My speeds and heights were all over the place, and I even made mistakes doing the familiar airfield departure. All the things I'd dreaded were really happening. The little voice in my brain that I'd tried not to listen to, that had told me I wasn't good enough, was being proved right. It was absolutely horrible! Indeed, after a few minutes I almost told the examiner that we should abandon the test, for I thought that we might as well, since I was quite sure that I'd failed anyway.

But I didn't. For I suddenly remembered something that made me stop panicking and manage to start, albeit rather shakily, to pull myself together. My instructor, knowing my problem with nerves, had reminded me that examiner's discretion was an important part of the test. He said that there may be particular things you're meant to do or not do, but ultimately it is all down to the examiner. Therefore you should not pre-judge the issue, and never give up till it's all over.

With that in mind, I resolved to give the thing my best shot. I decided that it didn't matter if I passed or failed. I'd just fly, and to hell with what happened! I'd treat it as a learning experience, and if necessary I'd take the test again at a later date. Almost immediately, things began to get better. Not instantaneously, fantastically, wonderfully better, for there are no miracles in aviation. But my numbing panic eased somewhat. And this meant that I could fly, probably just about as well or badly as I normally did.

The first section was navigation, and despite the bad start and by now being way off track, I managed to correct my heading. I found the isolated house I'd been given as a grid reference – though I was still so scared that I could hardly get the words out to tell the examiner which house I thought it was. And the rest of that section went tolerably well.

Then came the general handling. I was gradually calming down, and by now I was flying pretty much as I always did – though I still made a few more mistakes than usual, and forgot fairly simple things. Finally there was the instrument flying. I had always enjoyed that, and I managed to just relax and do everything I was supposed to. That section went rather well, I thought to myself. What a pity it was too late – since I was quite certain I'd failed. I couldn't see how any examiner could pass me after the hash I'd made of the first part of the test.

But I was wrong. Over a cup of coffee, the examiner told me that it had been obvious that I was incredibly nervous at the beginning. However, he said, he had been impressed by the fact that I'd gradually managed to overcome my nerves, and that I got better, not worse, as some people did in such situations. And, he said, I'd proved I could navigate … in the end. My general handling had been of an acceptable standard after the early errors, and he thought that my instrument flying was very good (wow!). He finished this long debrief by saying 'So you've passed, but I don't want you to think you did well.' I breathed a massive sigh of relief, and said, 'I know I didn't do well'.

The moral of this story is something I said earlier, but it should always be remembered. No matter what happens in a flight test, never ever give up.

And now, good luck for the test, and in all your future flying, wherever you go and whatever you fly.

Good luck in all your future flying!

Useful Addresses

Aircraft Owners and Pilots Association (AOPA)
50A Cambridge Street
London
SW1V 4QQ
0207 834 5631
www.aopa.co.uk

British Women Pilots'Association (BWPA)
Brooklands Museum
Brooklands Road
Weybridge
Surrey
KT13 0QN
www.bwpa.co.uk

Civil Aviation Authority (CAA)
Safety Regulation Group
Aviation House
Gatwick Airport South
West Sussex
RH6 0YR
01293 573700
www.caa.co.uk

General Aviation Safety Council (GASCo)
Rochester Airport
Chatham
Kent
ME5 9SD
www.gasco.org.uk

Guild of Air Pilots and Air Navigators (GAPAN)
Cobham House
9 Warwick Court
Gray's Inn
London
WC1R 5DJ
0207 404 4032
www.gapan.org

Helicopter Association International (HAI)
1635 Prince Street
Alexandria
Virginia 22314 2818
USA
(+001) 703 683 4646
www.rotor.com

Helicopter Club of Great Britain (HCGB)
Ryelands House
Aynho
Banbury
Oxon OX17 3AT
www.hcgb.co.uk

The Helicopter Museum
75 Elm Tree Road
Locking
Weston-Super-Mare
Avon
BS24 8EL
01934 822524
www.helicoptermuseum.co.uk

Met Office
Fitzroy Road
Exeter
Devon
EX1 3PB
0870 900 0100
www.metoffice.com

Royal Aeronautical Society (RAeS)
4 Hamilton Place
London
W1V 0BQ
0207 799 3515
www.raes.ork.uk

INDEX

RELATED TITLES FROM CROWOOD

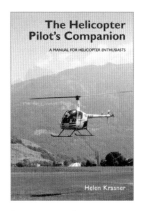

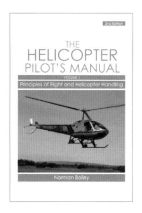

The Helicopter Pilot's Companion
A Manual for Helicopter Enthusiasts
Helen Krasner
ISBN 978 1 84797 049 7
160pp, 28 illustrations

The Helicopter Pilot's Manual Vol. 1
Principles of Flight and Helicopter Handling
Norman Bailey
ISBN 978 1 86126 982 9
256pp, 130 illustrations

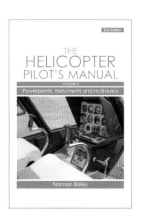

The Helicopter Pilot's Manual Vol. 2
Powerplants, Instruments and Hydraulics
Norman Bailey
ISBN 978 1 86126 991 1
176pp, 118 illustrations

The Helicopter Pilot's Manual Vol. 3
Mountain Flying and Advanced Techniques
Norman Bailey
ISBN 978 1 84797 105 0
128pp, 138 illustrations